133

New York

D0995619

COLLINS

Glasgow & London

First published 1990
Copyright © William Collins Sons & Company Limited
Printed and Published by
William Collins Sons & Company Limited
ISBN 0 00 435782-5

HOW TO USE THIS BOOK

Your Collins Traveller Guide will help you find your way around your chosen destination quickly and easily. It is colour-coded for easy reference:

The blue-coded 'topic' section answers the question 'I would like to see or do something; where do I go and what do I see when I get there?' A simple, clear layout provides an alphabetical list of activities and events, offers you a selection of each, tells you how to get there, what it will cost, when it is open and what to expect. Each topic in the list has its own simplified map, showing the position of each item and the nearest landmark or transport access, for instant orientation. Whether your interest is Architecture or Sport you can find all the information you need quickly and simply. Where major resorts within an area require in-depth treatment, they follow the main topics section in alphabetical order.

The red-coded section is a lively and informative gazetteer. In one alphabetical list you can find essential facts about the main places and cultural items - 'What is La Bastille?', 'Who was Michelangelo?' - as well as practical and invaluable travel information. It covers everything you need to know to help you enjoy yourself and get the most out of your time away, from Accommodation through Babysitters, Car Hire, Food, Health, Money, Newspapers, Taxis and Telephones to Zoos.

Cross-references: Type in small capitals - CHURCHES - tells you that more information on an item is available within the topic on churches. A-Z in bold - **A-Z** - tells you that more information is available on an item within the gazetteer. Simply look under the appropriate heading. A name in bold - **Holy Cathedral** - also tells you that more information on an item is available in the gazetteer under that particular heading.

Packed full of information and easy to use - you'll always know where you are with your Collins Traveller Guide!

Photographs by **Douglas Corrance**

INTRODUCTION

Descriptions of New York can read like the boastings of a small boy - the reader is left knee-deep in superlatives. If one word could sum up New York it would be 'contrasts'. New York is full of them. The most modern buildings - awesome feats of design and engineering, graceful, beautiful, occasionally humorous, sometimes ugly - share the streets of midtown Manhattan with lavishly ornamented 19th-century blocks built on a human scale where, from street level, you can see the people on the top floor. Within a bus ride of this modern metropolis are rows of 18th-century houses - in Greenwich Village - which could be part of a small prosperous rural town.

The most beautiful cities are those you feel you want to walk around in. New York will make you feel you want to walk as often as you can. We have suggested four walks, but if you have time you will discover others, either on your own or in the company of one of the city's many tour guides, who will share their love and knowledge of their city. If you have time in New York for only one walk, choose the one which interests you most and let the people of New York show you around. Do not be afraid to ask for help or information. Except at rush hours, when they want out of the maelstrom just as much as you, New Yorkers will have time to answer your questions and tell you a little about themselves as well. They love their city and they will love you for showing an interest in it.

In daytime New York is as safe as any other modern city, and much safer than many others in the US. At night do not flaunt your wealth or study your street map at every corner and no harm will come to you. The police may look fearsome but they are as friendly as any other man or woman on the street. If you feel the need to travel any distance, stay at street level and take the bus. They are much safer and simpler to understand than the subways, and they are cleaner, quieter and much more comfortable. The driver knows where he is going and he will help you find where you want to go. One dollar in change (no notes and no pennies - one cent coins) or a subway token, which are worth buying even if you do not use the subway, will take you anywhere in Manhattan. The driver will give you a transfer ticket for an intersecting bus route. The taxi drivers do not know where they are going - although they drive as if they do - and nowadays many do not speak

fluent English so you cannot tell them where you want to go - unless your Spanish is good.

New York will not disappoint you. It has something for everyone. Even if you do not like modern cities you can visit Central Park and delight in the design of Olmsted and Vaux and its execution by Pilat in creating a rural paradise which holds the urban giant at bay. New York City is enormous, but it is only a tiny part of New York State. Within the city Manhattan takes precedence, but it is only one borough in five. There are two urban boroughs - the Bronx and Brooklyn - and the suburban and rural boroughs of Queens and Staten Island.

Look on New York as your own personal 'new frontier' and become an explorer. Every block will have something to reward the adventurous spirit. It does not seem to matter that the world has been there before you; shopkeepers and shop assistants, bartenders, gallery staff, restaurant owners and waiters, all will welcome you as if you were the first. If you find all this goodwill a bit overpowering have a break at a New York deli. The contrast here is in the offhand attitude of the waiters. It is the tradition of deli waiters to treat everyone with brusque disdain. It's not just you and your unfamiliarity with the myriad choices of the menu. They do it to everyone.

You should try to visit a New York deli - for the experience - but you have an overwhelming choice of menus in New York; enough to sample a different cuisine every day for more than three weeks! While New York has some of the best (and the most expensive) restaurants in the world, you can also eat your fill of good food for very little cost. If you plan to walk all day you will need a substantial breakfast - the choice and the portions are huge. For a break at lunchtime try a 'sandwich to go' - they are big enough to share, and if you don't mind eating in the street, no one else will. To recharge your batteries at night try Chinatown without any fear of draining your cash reserves.

You can 'shop till you drop' - if you have the cash or the credit. This is the city that made shopping a career. Some shops may be well beyond your price range, but visit them anyway - for the experience, and the name. You needn't buy anything - looking is still free - and you will be able to say, 'When I was in Bloomingdale's…', or Macy's, or Tiffany's. There are shops in New York to suit every taste, age and bank account. You will find discount shops where the prices of good quality goods are amazingly low. Give New York time and you will find exactly what you want at the right price.

When you have had enough of Fifth Avenue shops, you can feast your eyes on some of the best art collections in the world. You will find an unrivalled range in the Metropolitan Museum (the Met), the Museum of Modern Art (MOMA), the Guggenheim, the Whitney and the beautiful Frick Collection - this gallery is a work of art in its own right.

After pounding the pavements you may want to sit back and be entertained. New York is the city where show business was born. All tastes from the highest to the lowest are catered for and some of the best is free. No summer visitor with an afternoon and evening to spare (except Monday) should miss 'Shakespeare in the Park'. The Theater District, around Broadway and 42nd Street, and its 'suburbs', Off-Broadway and Off-Off-Broadway, will add to your experience without necessarily costing you a week's wages, although you could pay this if you just *must* see the latest Broadway hit musical. If the straight theatre is too straight for you, the bars, cabarets and music clubs will have you laughing, singing or dancing - perhaps all three at once. Should something more refined be required the Lincoln Center and Carnegie Hall will offer you a full choice.

Eating, travelling by bus or subway and entertaining yourself in New York can be cheap, but good accommodation in Manhattan is expensive. If your funds are limited but your tolerance, and that of your friends, is unlimited, share an apartment and spend your money on

enjoying New York, and not just living in New York.

The best time to visit the city is the autumn. The winter is very cold but short, the spring is cool and wet and the summers are long, hot and humid. If you have no choice, fear not, New York and its people will compensate for the weather. Where the Statue of Liberty once welcomed the 'poor huddled masses', she now welcomes tourists. All that Liberty and the citizens of New York ask of you is that you do two things - 'enjoy, enjoy!'. You may have enjoyed your visits to other great cities, but New York is much more than just the sights, sounds and tastes of a great city. New York is an experience you will never forget.

Paul Gunnion

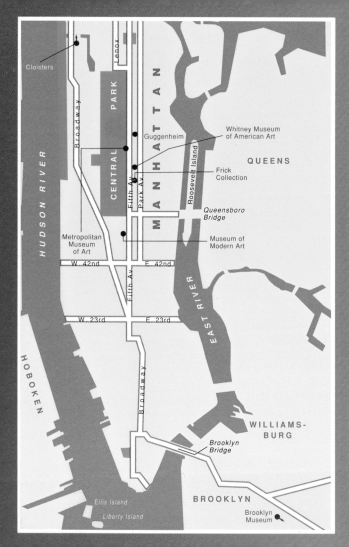

BROOKLYN MUSEUM 200 Eastern Parkway, Brooklyn.
• 1000-1700 Wed.-Mon. **S** 2-4 to Eastern Parkway/Brooklyn Museum.
• $2, student $1.50, accompanied child under 12 free.
One of America's leading museums of art.

FRICK COLLECTION 1 E 70th St.
• 1000-1800 Tues.-Sat., 1300-1800 Sun., closed hol.
Bus M1-M4. **S** 6 to 68th St./Hunter College/Lexington Av.
• $2 Tues.-Sat., $3 Sun., student $0.50.
If you choose only one museum to visit this should be the one. See **A-Z**.

GUGGENHEIM MUSEUM Fifth Av at 89th St.
• 1100-1700 Wed.-Sun., 1100-2000 Tues. Bus M1-M4, M18. **S** 4-6 to
86th St. • $4, student $2, free after 1700 Tues.
Modern art in an extravagant building by Frank Lloyd Wright. See **A-Z**.

METROPOLITAN MUSEUM OF ART Fifth Av at 82nd St.
• 0930-1715 Wed.-Sun., 0930-2045 Tues. Bus M1-M4. **S** 4-6 to 86th
St./Lexington Av. • $5, student $2.50 (includes Cloisters - see below).
Remarkable art collection. Free daily highlights tour. See **WALK 1**, **A-Z**.

CLOISTERS Fort Tryon Park.
Bus M4, M100. **S** A to 190th St. • See Metropolitan Museum of Art.
Contains a vast collection of medieval art. See **A-Z**.

MUSEUM OF MODERN ART (MOMA) 11 W 53rd St.
• 1100-1800 Fri.-Tues., 1100-2100 Thurs. Bus M1-M5. **S** E, F to 53rd
St./Fifth Av; B, D, S, F to Rockefeller Center.
• $5, student $3.50, donation Thurs.
Favourite meeting place of wealthy New Yorkers. Pleasing setting. See **A-Z**.

WHITNEY MUSEUM OF AMERICAN ART 945 Madison Av at
75th St.
• 1100-1700 Wed.-Sat., 1200-1800 Sun., 1300-2000 Tues.
Bus M1-M4, M30. **S** 6 to 77th St. • $4, free after 1800 Tues.
Houses comprehensive collections of American art. See **WALK 3**, **A-Z**.

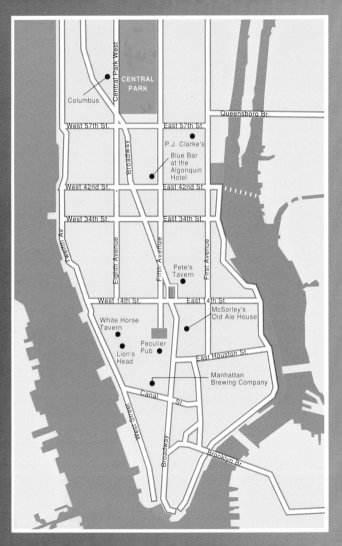

See **Opening Times**.

BLUE BAR AT THE ALGONQUIN HOTEL 59 W 44th St.

Bus M27, M104, M106. S B, D, F to 42nd St.; 7 to Fifth Av.

Dim, romantic and cosy - attracting indiscreet celebrities.

COLUMBUS 201 Columbus Av at 69th St.

Bus M11, M7. S B, C, 1-3 to 72nd St.; 1 to Lincoln Center.

Another good place for celebrity spotting. A favourite with Woody Allen.

LION'S HEAD 59 Christopher St. off Sheridan Sq.

Bus M5, M6, M10. S 1 to Christopher St./Sheridan Sq.

NYC's writers' pub - the place to come if you have any literary pretensions.

MANHATTAN BREWING COMPANY 40 Thompson St. at Watts St.

Bus M5, M6, M10, M21. S A, C, E, K to Canal St.

Hard-to-find beers from all over the US, plus some brewed on the premises.

McSORLEY'S OLD ALE HOUSE 15 E Seventh St.

Bus M15, M101, M102, M13. S 6 to Astor Pl.

One of the the city's oldest pubs (women used to be barred!). Good beer.

PECULIER PUB 145 Bleecker St. between Thompson St. & La Guardia.

Bus M2, M3. S A-F to Washington Sq.

Selection of over 200 beers from all over the world.

PETE'S TAVERN 129 E 18th St. at Irving Pl.

Bus M101, M102. S L, N, R, 4-6 to Union Sq.

The oldest bar in NYC. An air of simplicity and quiet prevails.

P. J. CLARKE'S 915 Third Av at 55th St.

Bus M1-M4, M32, M101, M102. S E, F to Lexington Av.

A classic, old, Irish saloon bar. Good at any time, but best late at night.

WHITE HORSE TAVERN 567 Hudson St. at W 11th St.

Bus M10, M11, M14. S A, C, E to 14th St.; 1 to Christopher St.

Dylan Thomas had his last drink here. Good jukebox. Street café in summer.

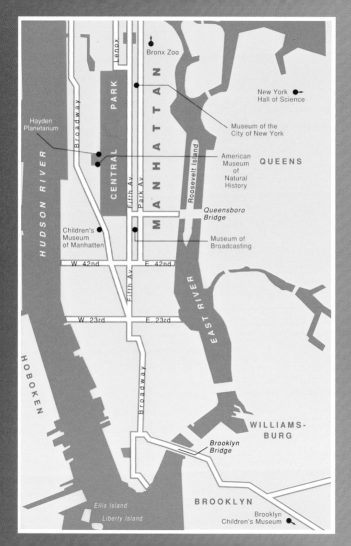

AMERICAN MUSEUM OF NATURAL HISTORY Central Park.
•1000-1745 Mon., Tues., Thurs., Sun.; 1000-2100 Wed., Fri., Sat. Bus
M10, M17. S A-C, K to 81st St. •$3.50, child $1.50, free 1700 Fri., Sat.
Especially famous for its extensive collection of dinosaur bones. See A-Z.

BRONX ZOO Bronx River Parkway at Fordham Rd.
•1000-1700 (till 1730 Sun.) Feb.-Oct., 1000-1630 Nov.-Jan. S 2, 5 to
E 180th St. •$3.75, child $1.50 Fri.-Mon.; donation Tues.-Thurs.
Children's zoo where they can learn all about animals. See Zoos.

BROOKLYN CHILDREN'S MUSEUM 145 Brooklyn Av.
•1000-1700 Wed.-Mon. S 2-4 to Eastern P'kway/Br'klyn Mus. •Donation.
World's first children's museum - opportunities to join in as well as to look.

CHILDREN'S MUSEUM OF MANHATTAN 314 W 54th St.
•1000-1900 Tues.-Sat., 1300-1900 Sun.
Bus M7, M11, M18, M104. S S 57th St.
Activities include constructing a tepee or fashioning a flute.

HAYDEN PLANETARIUM Central Park West at 81st St.
•Opening times and prices vary. Bus M10, M17. S B, C, K to 81st St.
Sky shows and laser spectaculars accompanied by rock music. See A-Z.

MUSEUM OF BROADCASTING 1 E 53rd St.
•1200-1700 Tues.-Sat. Bus M1-M4, M27, M32. S B, D, F to Rockefeller
Center. •$4, child and senior citizen $2, student $3.
Watch favourite TV shows from the archives (go early for the best choice).

MUSEUM OF THE CITY OF NEW YORK Fifth Av at 103rd St.
•1000-1700 Tues.-Sat., 1300-1700 Sun. & hol.
Bus M1-M4, M19. S 6 to 103rd St. •Free.
Toy gallery, antique fire engines, Big Apple slide show. See MUSEUMS 1.

NEW YORK HALL OF SCIENCE 47-01 111th St., Queens.
•1100-1800 Wed.-Sun. S 7 to 111th St. •$2.50, child $1.50.
Hands-on fun - why cats' eyes glow in the dark and what electricity is.

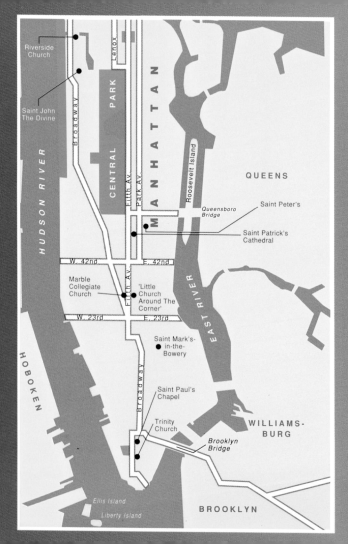

Riverside
Church

Saint John
The Divine

Lenox

CENTRAL PARK

MANHATTAN

Roosevelt Island

QUEENS

HUDSON RIVER

Broadway

Fifth Av.

Park Av.

Queensboro
Bridge

Saint Peter's

Saint Patrick's
Cathedral

W. 42nd   E. 42nd

Marble
Collegiate
Church

Fifth Av.

'Little
Church
Around The
Corner'

EAST RIVER

W. 23rd   E. 23rd

Saint Mark's-
in-the-
Bowery

HOBOKEN

Broadway

Saint Paul's
Chapel

Trinity
Church

Brooklyn
Bridge

WILLIAMS-
BURG

Ellis Island

Liberty Island

BROOKLYN

'LITTLE CHURCH AROUND THE CORNER' 29th St. E of Fifth Av.
Bus M2, M3, M32. S N, R to 28th St./Broadway.
*A favourite with theatre people. Has a certain country-cottage appeal which makes it popular for weddings. See **A-Z**.*

MARBLE COLLEGIATE CHURCH Fifth Av at 29th St.
Bus M2, M3, M32. S N, R to 28th St./Broadway.
*The oldest Protestant church in the USA (founded in 1628). See **A-Z**.*

RIVERSIDE CHURCH 122nd St. at Riverside Dr.
Bus M5. S 1 to 125th St.
*Climb the tower for good views of the city (costs $0.25). See **A-Z**.*

ST JOHN THE DIVINE 112th St. at Amsterdam Av.
Bus M4, M11. S A-C, K, 1 to Cathedral Parkway/110th St.
*The largest Gothic cathedral in the world (still unfinished). See **A-Z**.*

ST MARK'S-IN-THE-BOWERY Second Av at Tenth St.
Bus M15. S 4-6 to 14th St./Union Sq.
*Busy community church. Readings and concerts. See **A-Z**.*

ST PATRICK'S CATHEDRAL Fifth Av at 50th St.
Bus M1-M5, M27. S B, D, F to Rockefeller Center.
*Large Gothic cathedral with a splendid interior. See **A-Z**.*

ST PAUL'S CHAPEL Broadway at Fulton St.
Bus M1, M6. S A, C, J, M, R, 2-5 to Fulton St./Broadway.
*The oldest church in Manhattan (1766). See **WALK 4**, **A-Z**.*

ST PETER'S Lexington Av at 54th St.
Bus M101, M102. S E, F to Lexington Av/53rd St.
*Lutheran church which has become part of the Citicorp Center (see **A-Z**).*

TRINITY CHURCH Broadway at Wall St.
Bus M1, M6. S 4, 5 to Wall St./Broadway.
*Small church with its own museum. See **WALK 4**, **A-Z**.*

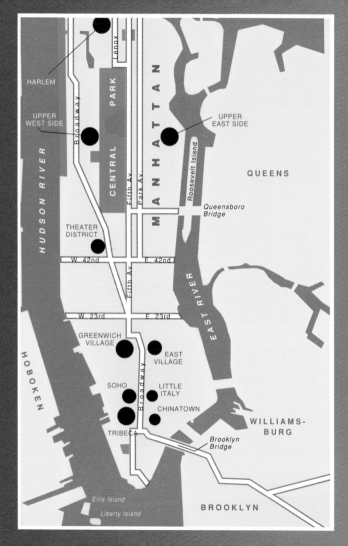

UPPER WEST SIDE Central Park West to the Hudson River, 59th St. to 90th St.
Bus M5, M7, M10, M11, M17, M18, M30, M104. S 1 to 79th St.
Up-market residential area containing boutiques, cafés and bars.

CHINATOWN/LITTLE ITALY Canal St. to East Broadway, Bowery St. to Centre St./Canal St. to Kenmore St., Centre St. to Bowery St.
Bus M1, M6, M101, M102. S B, D, J, M, N, Q, R, 4, 6 to Canal St.
Two areas which have almost merged geographically. Hundreds of Chinese and Italian restaurants and shops. See **A-Z**.

GREENWICH VILLAGE 14th St. to Houston St., west of Broadway to the Hudson River.
Bus M1, M5, M6, M10. S E, F to W Fourth St.; 3 to Christopher St.
Bars, restaurants, shops. Great for street life. See **WALK 2**, **A-Z**.

HARLEM 96th St. to 168th St., the Hudson River to the Harlem River.
Bus M1, M2, M7, M10, M102. S A-D, 2, 3 to 125th St.
Attractions include Hamilton Grange (see **A-Z***), Grant's Tomb (see* **A-Z***), the Cloisters (see* **ART GALLERIES**, **A-Z***) and Audubon Terrace (see* **A-Z***). See* **A-Z**.

SOHO/TRIBECA Houston St. to Chambers St., Br'dway to the Hudson.
Bus M1, M5, M6, M10. S B, E, J, M, N to Canal St.; 4, 6 to Spring St.
Admire the cast-iron buildings (see **A-Z***) and historic landmarks. See* **A-Z**.

THEATER DISTRICT 42nd St. to 59th St., Seventh Av to the Hudson.
Bus M6, M7, M10, M104. S A-C, K, N, Q-S, 1-3, 7 to 42nd St.
Busy 24 hr a day. Most Broadway shows are staged here. See **Theatre**.

UPPER EAST SIDE 59th St. to 96th St., Fifth Av to the East River.
Bus M1-M4, M15, M101, M102. S 4-6 to 77th St.
Famous people reside in this patrician district. Lively nightlife.

EAST VILLAGE Broadway to Av D, Houston St. to 14th St.
Bus M13, M15, M101, M102. S F to Houston St.
Slightly seedy home of punks, artists and East Europeans. See **A-Z**.

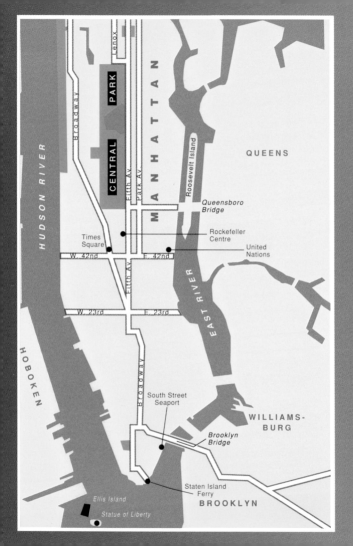

CENTRAL PARK
Bus M1-M4, M30 on Fifth Av; M5-M7, M103 on 59th St.; M17-M19, M29 through Central Park. S B, N, R to Fifth Av.
840 acres of greenery in the middle of Manhattan. See **PARKS**, **WALK 1**, **A-Z**.

ELLIS ISLAND
Bus M1, M6. S 1 to South Ferry. Circle Line Ferry from Battery Park.
Former immigration centre and gateway to America for the 16 million 'huddled masses yearning to breathe free'. Temporarily closed. See **A-Z**.

ROCKEFELLER CENTER 48th St. to 52nd St., Fifth Av to Seventh Av.
Bus M5-M7. S B, D, F, S to Rockefeller Center.
Prestigious 22-acre complex featuring 19 Art Deco buildings. See **A-Z**.

SOUTH STREET SEAPORT South St.
Bus M15, M23. S A, C, J, M, R, 2-5 to Fulton St./William St.
The 19thC port district with bars, shops and restaurants. See **WALK 4**, **A-Z**.

STATEN ISLAND FERRY South Ferry.
Bus M1, M6. S 1 to South Ferry. •$0.25 return (avoid at rush hour).
Views of Manhattan, the Statue of Liberty, Ellis Island (see **A-Z***). See* **A-Z**.

STATUE OF LIBERTY Liberty Island.
•0900-1600. Bus M1, M6. S 1 to South Ferry. Circle Line Ferry from Battery Park.
Symbol of American freedom and the American Dream. See **A-Z**.

TIMES SQUARE 42nd to 47th St., Broadway to Seventh Av.
Bus M6, M7. S B, D, N, Q-S, 1-3, 7 to Times Sq.
Former home of the New York Times *(see* **Newspapers***). See* **WALK 3**, **A-Z**.

UNITED NATIONS First Av between 42nd St. & 48th St.
•0930-1645. Bus M15, M104, M106. S S, 4-7 to 42nd St./Grand Central. •$4.50, child $2.50 (no pre-school-age children allowed).
Famous complex along the East River (see **A-Z***), where the heads of governments meet to discuss global issues. See* **WALK 3**, **A-Z**.

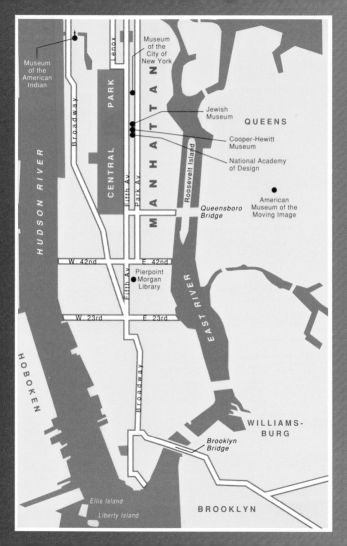

PIERPOINT MORGAN LIBRARY 29 E 36th St. at Madison Av.
• 1030-1700 Tues.-Sat., 1300-1700 Sun., closed Aug. & Sun. in July.
Bus M1, M2, M3, M32. S 6 to 33rd St. •Donation.
*Precious medieval manuscripts, rare books and works of art, including
Rembrandt prints. See* **A-Z**.

COOPER-HEWITT MUSEUM 2 E 91st St.
• 1000-1700 Wed.-Sat., 1000-2100 Tues., 1200-1700 Sun.
Bus M1-M4, M18, M19. S 4-6 to 86th St. •$3, free 1700-2100 Tues.
Changing exhibitions of decorative arts. See **A-Z**.

JEWISH MUSEUM Fifth Av at 92nd St.
• 1200-1700 Mon.-Thurs., 1200-2000 Tues., 1100-1800 Sun. Bus M1-
M4, M19. S 6 to 96th St. •$3; student, child, senior citizen $1.50.
Large collection of religious objects, cultural artefacts and modern Jewish art.

MUSEUM OF THE AMERICAN INDIAN Broadway at 155th St.
• 1000-1700 Tues.-Sat., 1300-1700 Sun. Bus M4, M5, BX6.
S 1 to 157th St. •$2, student $1.
Marvellous representation of Indian culture. Well worth visiting.

MUSEUM OF THE CITY OF NEW YORK Fifth Av at 103rd St.
• 1000-1700 Tues.-Sat., 1300-1700 Sun. & hol. Bus M1-M4, M19.
S 6 to 103rd St. •Free.
The 'Big Apple Show' is a good introduction to NY's history. See **CHILDREN**.

NATIONAL ACADEMY OF DESIGN Fifth Av at 89th St.
• 1200-1700 Wed.-Sun., 1200-2000 Tues. Bus M1-M4, M18. S 4-6 to
86th St. •$2.50, student and senior citizen $2, free 1700-2000 Tues.
19th and 20thC American portraiture, painting, sculpture, photography, etc.

AMERICAN MUSEUM OF THE MOVING IMAGE 36th St. at
35th Av, Astoria, Queens.
• 1000-2000 Sat., 1000-1700 Sun., 1300-1700 Mon.-Thurs., 1300-
2000 Fri. S R to Steinway St. •$4, student and senior citizen $2.
Memorabilia and high-tech exhibits tracing the history of film.

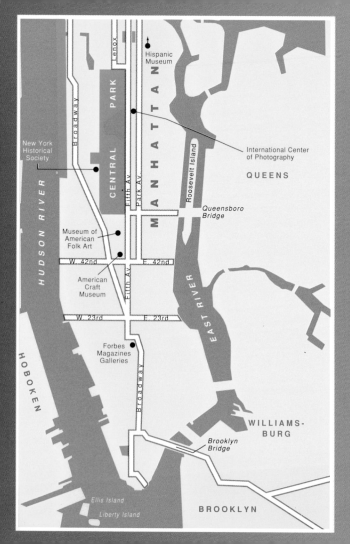

AMERICAN CRAFT MUSEUM 40 W 53rd St. at Fifth Av.
•1000-2000 Tues., 1000-1700 Wed., Sun. Bus M1-M4, M27, M32. S B, D, F, S to Rockefeller Center. •$3.50, student $1.50, free after 1700 Tues.
Permanent collection of the best of 20thC American crafts, sponsored by the American Craft Council, plus interesting temporary exhibitions.

FORBES MAGAZINES GALLERIES 62 Fifth Av at 12th St.
•1000-1600 Tues., Wed., Fri., Sat.
Bus M2, M3, M5. S B, D, L, N, Q, R, 4-6 to Union Sq. •Free.
Exhibits include toy boats and soldiers, and the largest collection of Fabergé Easter eggs in the world.

HISPANIC MUSEUM Broadway & 155th St.
•1000-1630 Tues.-Sat., 1300-1600 Sun.
Bus M104. S 1 to Broadway/157th St. •$2.50.
Wonderful display of Spanish art and artefacts. Paintings by El Greco, Velázquez and Goya. See **A-Z**.

INTERNATIONAL CENTER OF PHOTOGRAPHY 1130 Fifth Av.
•1200-1700 Wed.-Fri., 1200-2000 Tues., 1100-1800 Sat.-Sun.
Bus M19, M101, M102. S 6 to Lexington Av/96th St.
•$2.50, free after 1700 Tues.
Permanent display of works by Cartier-Bresson, Adams and Kertesz in this elegant, early-20thC town house. Good temporary exhibitions.

MUSEUM OF AMERICAN FOLK ART 125 W 55th St. between Sixth Av & Seventh Av.
•1030-1730 Wed.-Sun. (till 2000 Tues.). Bus M5-M7. S B, D, N, Q, R to 57th St./Seventh Av. •$2; student, senior citizen $1; free 1730-2000 Tues.
Early American hand-crafted quilts, toys, signs, decoys, weather vanes, etc.

NEW YORK HISTORICAL SOCIETY Central Park West at 77th St.
•1100-1700 Tues.-Sat., 1300-1700 Sun. S B, C, K to 81st St.
•$3, child $1.
The city's oldest museum, founded in 1804, exhibits American folk art, colonial artefacts, antique toys, old prints and maps and coaches. See **A-Z**.

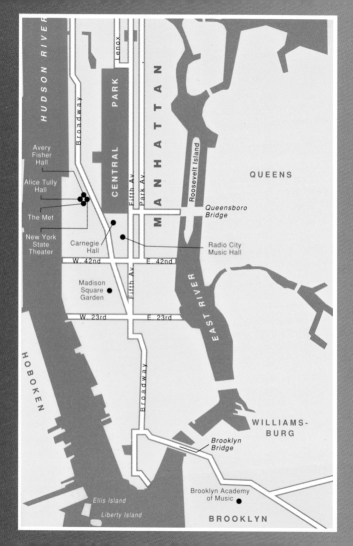

ALICE TULLY HALL Lincoln Center, Broadway at 64th St.
Bus M5, M7, M29, M30, M104. S 1 to Lincoln Center.
Chamber music, recitals and string quartets. See **Lincoln Center**.

AVERY FISHER HALL Lincoln Center, Broadway at 64th St.
Bus M5, M7, M29, M30, M104. S 1 to Lincoln Center.
Home of the NY Philharmonic, directed by Mehta. See **Lincoln Center**.

BROOKLYN ACADEMY OF MUSIC (BAM) 30 Lafayette St.
S G to Fulton St.
The oldest performing-arts academy in the US. Legendary figures such as Isadora Duncan and Gertrude Stein have appeared here. See **A-Z**.

CARNEGIE HALL 154 W 57th St.
Bus M5-M7. S S to 57th St.
The acoustics are better than ever after a $50 million renovation. All the greats have played here, from Mahler to Sinatra and Holiday. See **A-Z**.

MADISON SQUARE GARDEN Seventh Av at 33rd St.
Bus M4, M10, M16. S 1-3 to Penn Station.
Venue for superstars like Michael Jackson and Bruce Springsteen. See **A-Z**.

METROPOLITAN OPERA HOUSE (THE MET) Lincoln Center,
Broadway at 64th St.
Bus M5, M7, M29, M30, M104. S 1 to Lincoln Center.
Home of the Metropolitan Opera Company (Sept.-Apr.) and the American Ballet Theater (May-June). Chagall murals in the lobby. See **Lincoln Center**.

NEW YORK STATE THEATER Lincoln Center, Broadway at 64th St.
Bus M5, M7, M29, M30, M104. S 1 to Lincoln Center.
Where the New York City Ballet performs. See **Lincoln Center**.

RADIO CITY MUSIC HALL 50th St. & Sixth Av.
Bus M1-M4, M27, M32. S B, D, F, S to Rockefeller Center.
Largest indoor music hall. Pop and rock concerts by groups ranging from The Grateful Dead to The Temptations. See **Rockefeller Center**.

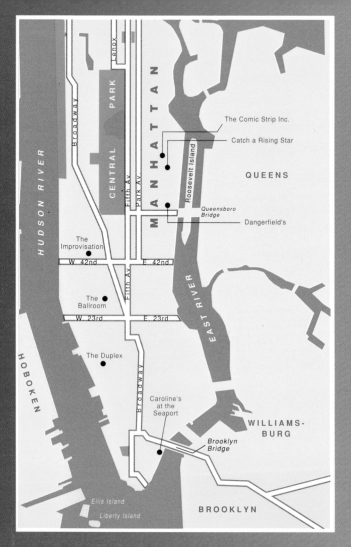

Comedy

CAROLINE'S AT THE SEAPORT 89 South St.
•1700-0300 Wed.-Sat. Bus M15, M23. S A, C, J, M, 2, 3-5 to
Broadway/Nassau St./Fulton St.
•Cover charge varies, 2-drink minimum.
Features top new comedians such as Emo Philips.

CATCH A RISING STAR 1487 First Av at 77th St.
•2100 Sun.-Thurs., 2030 Fri., 1930 Sat. (first shows). Bus M15. S 6 to
77th St./Lexington Av. •$7 Sun.-Thurs., $12 Fri.-Sat., 2-drink minimum.
Showcase for new talent. Occasional return of an established star.

THE BALLROOM 253 W 29th St. between 7th Av & 8th Av.
•1830, 2100, 2300 Wed.-Sat.; 2100 Tues. Bus M10. S 1 to 28th St.
•Cover charge varies, 2-drink minimum.
Popular singers appear regularly. Sample the Spanish tapas (snacks).

THE COMIC STRIP INC. 1568 Second Av between 81st St. & 82nd St.
•2100. Bus M15, M17. S 4-6 to 86th St. •Cover charge varies, 2-drink
minimum.
Many of the greats were discovered here, Eddie Murphy for one.

DANGERFIELD'S 1118 First Av at South Park Av.
•2115 Sun.-Thurs.; 2100, 2330 Fri.; 2000, 2230, 0030 Sat.
Bus M15, M31, M103. S 4-6 to 59th St./Lexington Av. •$7 minimum.
Founded by the famous comedy star. He introduces newcomers nightly.

THE DUPLEX 55 Grove St. between Seventh Av & Bleecker St.
•2000, 2200 Mon.-Thurs.; 2000, 2200, 2400 Fri.-Sat.; 1500, 1730,
2000, 2200 Sun. Bus M5, M6, M10, M13. S 1 to Christopher St./
Sheridan Sq. •Cover charge varies, 2-drink minimum.
Woody Allen, Joan Rivers and Rodney Dangerfield started out in cabaret here.

THE IMPROVISATION 358 W 44th St. at Ninth Av.
•2100 Sun.-Fri., 2000 Sat. (first show). Bus M10, M11, M16, M106.
S A, C, E, K to 42nd St./Eighth Av. •Cover charge varies.
Greats like Richard Pryor return here to pay tribute and try out new material.

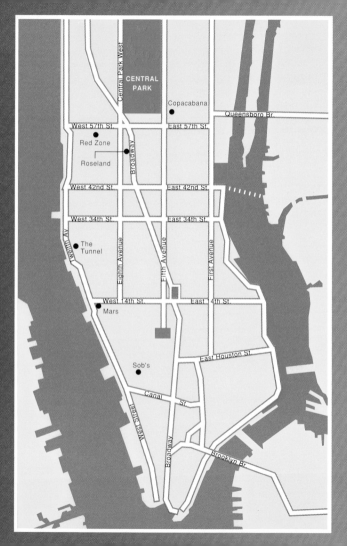

Discos

COPACABANA 10 E 60th St. near Fifth Av.
• From 1800. Bus M1-4, M103. S N, R to 60th St./Fifth Av.
• Cover charge varies.
Latin American and disco music. It's changed since Barry Manilow described it in song, but still packs 'em in.

MARS 28-30 Tenth Av at 14th St.
• 2200-0400. Bus M10, M11, M14. S A, C, E, L to 14th St./Eighth Av.
• Cover charge varies (capricious door policy).
Five dance floors featuring a variety of different kinds of music.

RED ZONE 440 W 54th St. between Ninth Av & Tenth Av.
• 2200-0400. Bus M10, M27, M104. S A-D, 1 to 59th St./Columbus Circle. • Cover charge varies.
One of the loudest disco-clubs in New York. Just the place for uninhibited partying.

ROSELAND 238 W 52nd St. between Seventh Av & Eighth Av.
• 1430-0500 Thurs.-Sun. Bus M6, M7, M10, M104.
S 1 to 50th St./Broadway. • Cover charge varies.
Ballroom dancing in the afternoons and evenings, disco late at night in this legendary establishment. Restaurant and bar.

SOB'S 204 Varick St. at W Houston St.
• 1900-0200 Tues.-Thurs., 1900-0400 Fri.-Sat. Bus M10, M21. S 1 to Houston St./Varick St. • Cover charge varies, 2-drink minimum.
Dance all night to the rhythms of Latin American, disco, jazz and salsa performed by live bands.

THE TUNNEL 220 12th Av at 27th St.
• 2100-0300. Bus M11, M26. S A, C, E to 23rd St./Eighth Av.
• Cover charge varies.
Popular disco in an intriguing location - a railway tunnel by the river. A spot for the fashionable and far-out. Plenty of places to relax in around the crowded main dance area.

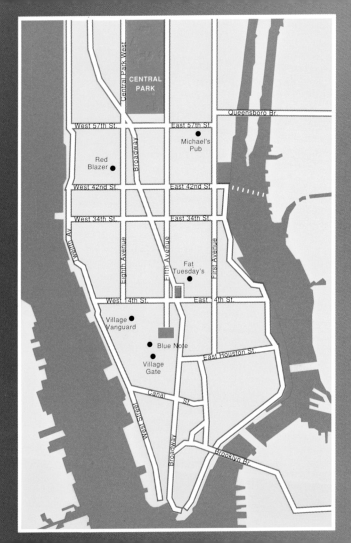

Jazz Clubs

BLUE NOTE 131 W Third St.
• 2100, 2330 Mon.-Thurs.; 2100, 2330, 0130 Fri.-Sat. Bus M2, M3, M5.
S A-F to W Fourth St./Washington Sq. •Cover charge varies at around
$25 per table, $15 at bar, $5 minimum.
*Expensive place to hear jazz greats and legends in the making. Jam here for
free after 0200.*

MICHAEL'S PUB 211 E 55th St. between Third Av & Second Av.
• 2100, 2300 Mon.-Sat. Bus M101, M102. S E, F to Lexington Av/
53rd St. •No cover charge, $10 minimum.
*Nostalgic jazz. Woody Allen plays the clarinet on Mondays when he is in
town.*

RED BLAZER 349 W 46th St. between Eighth Av & Ninth Av.
• 2100-0100. Bus M27, M104, M106. S A, C, E to 42nd St.
•No cover charge, no minimum.
Jazz spot featuring big bands and excellent Dixieland.

FAT TUESDAY'S 190 Third Av at 17th St.
• 2000, 2200 Tues.-Thurs.; 2000, 2200, 2400 Fri.-Sat. Bus M2, M7,
M102. S A-E, K to 125th St./St Nicholas Av; 2, 3 to 125th St./Lenox St.
•Cover charge varies, 2-drink minimum.
*Popular basement jazz club featuring known musicians. Bar and restaurant
at ground level.*

VILLAGE GATE Corner of Bleecker St. & Thompson St.
• 2130-0230. Bus M2, M3, M5. S A-F to W Fourth St./Washington Sq.
•Cover charge varies, $6 minimum.
*This club at the heart of the New York jazz scene is more like a hall. Bar
and café upstairs.*

VILLAGE VANGUARD 178 Seventh Av S at Perry St. & Waverly Pl.
• 2130, 2330, 0100. Bus M10. S 1 to Christopher St./Sheridan Sq.
•Cover charge varies around $15, 2-drink minimum.
*All the greats have played, and still come to play, at this jazz institution.
No food served.*

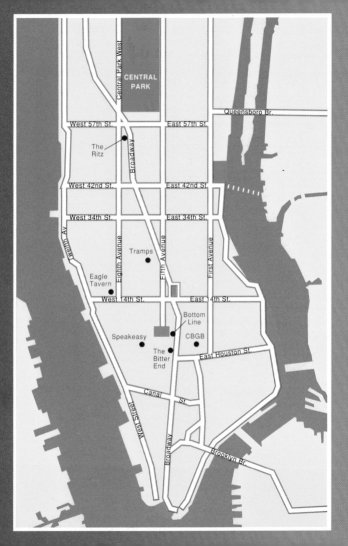

Music

THE BITTER END 147 Bleecker St.
•1700, show starts 2130. Bus M2, M3, M5. S A-F to W Fourth St./
Washington Sq. •Cover charge varies at around $5.
A showcase for some of the greatest when they were starting out. Features rock and other styles of music.

EAGLE TAVERN 355 W 14th St. between Eighth Av & Ninth Av.
•0800, show starts 2030. Bus M10, M11, M14. S A, C, E, L to 14th St./
Eighth Av. •$5, free Mon.
Folk venue where you can join in the party on Mondays. Wednesday is American folk night and Thursday is reserved for comedy.

BOTTOM LINE 15 W 4th St. at Mercer St.
•1900, shows at 2000, 2300. Bus M2, M3, M5. S A-F to W 4th St./
Washington Sq. •$12.50, no minimum.
Big name rock bands. Bruce Springsteen started out here.

THE RITZ 254 W 54th St. between Broadway & Eighth Av.
•1900, 2100-0400. Bus M10, M104. S A-D, 1 to 59th St./Columbus
Circle. •Cover charge varies.
Hosts the best in rock and R & B as well as unknowns getting their first break.

SPEAKEASY 107 MacDougal St.
•Nightly. Bus M2, M3, M5. S A-F, S to W Fourth St./Washington Sq.
Folk club with an open stage on Mondays when anyone can perform - the best come back and play again on Tuesday. Features big stars Wed.-Sat.

TRAMPS 45 W 21st St. between Fifth Av & Sixth Av.
•Nightly. Bus M2-M4. S N, R to 23rd St. •Cover charge varies.
Best place in NYC to listen to the blues. Rock and pop also get a hearing some nights of the week.

CBGB 315 Bowery at Bleecker St.
•Daily. Bus M15, M21, M101, M102. S F, S, 4, 6 to Bleecker St./
Lafayette St. •Cover charge varies at around $5.
This is where punks and heavy metal fans hang out.

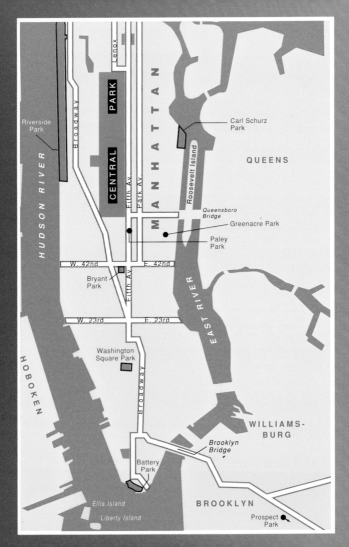

CENTRAL PARK From 59th St. to 110th St., Fifth Av to Central Park West.
Larger than the country of Monaco. See **CITY SIGHTS**, **WALK 1**, **A-Z**.

BRYANT PARK 42nd St. to Sixth Av.
Bus M5-M7. S B, D, F, S to 42nd St. Behind NY Public Library.
Second-hand book stalls and TKTS booth selling half-price tickets for same-day performances of music and dance (see **Theatre**). *See* **WALK 3**, **A-Z**.

CARL SCHURZ PARK East River, from 84th St. to 90th St.
Bus M18, M23, M31. S 4-6 to 86th St.
Watch the ships on the river, sunbathe, play basketball or jog.

RIVERSIDE PARK Hudson River, from 72nd St. to 158th St.
Bus M5. S 1 to 110th St.; 1 to 116th St.
Manhattan's second-largest park. Take a stroll beside the boat basin.

PROSPECT PARK Grand Army Plaza, Brooklyn.
S D to Prospect Pk; F to 15th St./Prospect Park; 2-4 to Grand Army Plaza.
Peace and tranquility of meadows, streams and a lake. Escape the bustle.

BATTERY PARK Southern tip of Manhattan.
Bus M1, M6. S 1 to Battery Park/South Ferry.
Small park with views of the harbour. See **WALK 4**, **A-Z**.

GREENACRE PARK 217 E 51st St.
Bus M5-M7. S B, D, F, S to Rockefeller Center.
Pocket handkerchief-sized paved plaza. Calm spot for reading or relaxing.

PALEY PARK E 53rd St. just off Fifth Av.
Bus M5-M7, M104, M106. S E, F Fifth Av/53rd St.
Tiny park with a waterfall and seats. See **A-Z**.

WASHINGTON SQUARE PARK W Fourth St. at Fifth Av.
Bus M2, M3, M5. S D to W Fourth St.
At the heart of Greenwich Village (see **CITY DISTRICTS**, **A-Z**). *See* **WALK 2**.

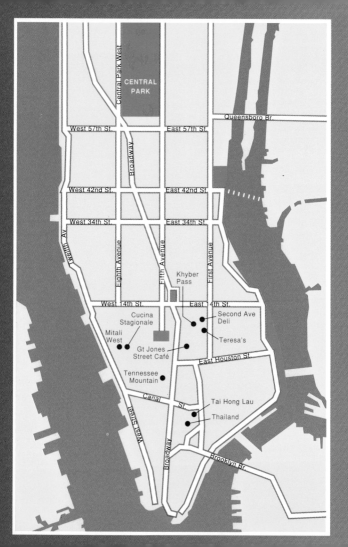

Downtown

CUCINA STAGIONALE 275 Bleecker St. between Jones & Morton St.
•Daily. Bus M5, M10, M12. S A-F to W Fourth St./Washington Sq.
Arrive early or you'll have to queue for the best deal in Italian food in town.

GT JONES ST. CAFÉ 54 Gt Jones St. between Br'dway & Bowery.
•Daily. Bus M1, M3, M5, M6. S B, D, F, 6 to Bleecker St./Lafayette St./
Broadway.
Popular with young people who patiently wait for delicious Cajun dishes.

KHYBER PASS 34 St Marks Pl between Second Av & Third Av.
•Daily. Bus M13, M15. S 6 to Astor Pl.
Delectable Afghan cuisine, traditional cushions and rugs, great prices.

SECOND AVENUE DELI 156 Second Av at Tenth St.
•Daily. Bus M15. S 6 to Astor Pl.
Downtown's favourite Jewish deli.

TAI HONG LAU 70 Mott St. between Canal St. & Bayard St.
•Daily. Bus M101, M102. S J, N, R, 6 to Canal St.
Exciting Cantonese food served in an elegant setting.

TERESA'S 103 First Av between Sixth St. & Seventh St.
•Daily. Bus M15. S 6 to Astor Pl.
Wonderful Polish dishes at exceptional prices.

THAILAND 106 Bayard St. at Baxter St. below Canal St.
•Daily. Bus M101, M102. S J, M, N, R, 6 to Canal St.
The best and the cheapest Thai food in NYC.

MITALI WEST 296 Bleecker St., corner of Seventh Av S & Barrow St.
•Daily. Bus M5, M10, M12. S A-F to W Fourth St./Washington Sq.
Wonderful food, attentive service, fantastic value.

TENNESSEE MOUNTAIN 143 Spring St. at corner of Wooster St.
•Daily. Bus M1, M6, M8. S 6 to Spring St.
Authentic 'down-home' barbecues in a charming old clapboard house.

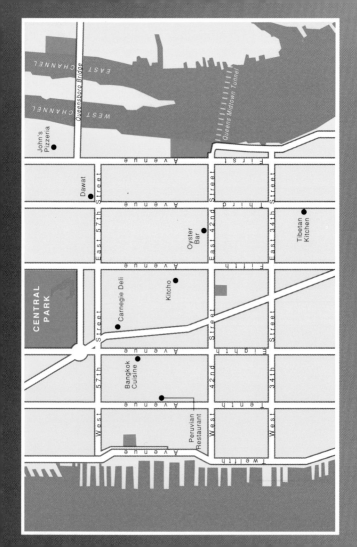

Midtown

BANGKOK CUISINE 885 Eighth Av between 52nd St. & 53rd St.
•1100-2300. Bus M10, M104. S C, E to 50th St./Eighth Av; 1 to 50th St./ Broadway.
Little known as yet, but one of the best Thai restaurants in the city.

CARNEGIE DELI 854 Seventh Av between 54th St. & 55th St.
•0630-0330. Bus M6, M7. S B, D, E to Seventh Av; N, R to Lexington Av.
An institution. Get to know the real New York in this popular Jewish deli.

JOHN'S PIZZERIA 408 E 64th St. between First Av & York Av.
•1130-2330 Mon.-Sat.,1200-2330 Sun. Bus M15, M23, M31. S N, R to Lexington Av; 4, 6 to 68th St./Lexington Av.
Delicious thin-crusted pizzas cooked in brick ovens. Dozens of toppings.

PERUVIAN RESTAURANT 688 Tenth Av at 48th St. & 49th St.
•1130-2330 Mon.-Sat., 1200-2330 Sun. Bus M11, M27. S C, E to 50th St./Eighth Av.
Try something different - tasty Peruvian dishes at unbeatable prices.

TIBETAN KITCHEN 144 Third Av between 30th St. & 31st St.
•1200-2330 Mon.-Sat. Bus M101, M102. S 4, 6 to 28th St./Park Av S.
Another exotic cuisine on offer in NYC. Well worth trying at these prices.

DAWAT 210 E 58th St. between Second Av & Third Av.
•1130-1500, 1730-2300 Mon.-Sat. (till 2330 Fri., Sat.); 1730-2300 Sun. Bus M29, M30, M101, M102. S N, R, 4-6 to 59th St./Lexington Av.
Good choice of imaginative Indian dishes. Menu devised by Madhur Jaffrey.

KITCHO 22 W 46th St. between Fifth Av & Sixth Av.
•1200-1430, 1800-2230 Mon.-Fri.; 1700-2230 Sun. Bus M1-M4, M32. S B, D, F to Rockefeller Center.
Japanese dishes cooked on red-hot rocks. The kaiseki dinners are excellent.

OYSTER BAR Grand Central Station, 42nd St. & Vanderbilt Av.
•1130-2130 Mon.-Fri. Bus M1-M4, M32, M104. S S, 4-7 to Gr'd Central.
Seafood restaurant serving the freshest fish in town. Spectacular setting.

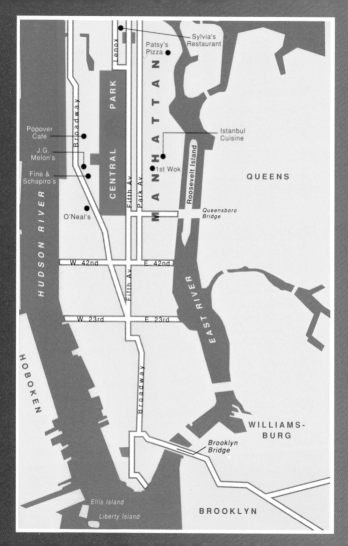

Uptown

FINE & SCHAPIRO'S 138 W 72nd St. between Broadway & Columbus Av.
•Daily. Bus M5, M7, M11, M30, M103, M104. S 1, 2 to 72nd St./Broadway.
A classic Jewish restaurant. The best on the West Side.

1ST WOK 1374 Third Av at 78th St.; 1570 Third Av between 88th St. & 89th St.; 1384 First Av at 74th St.
•Daily. Bus M17, M101, M102. S 6 to 77th St./Lexington Av.
Popular branches of a chain of Chinese restaurants serving Szechwan dishes.

ISTANBUL CUISINE 303 E 80th St. between First Av & Second Av.
•Daily. Bus M15, M17. S 6 to 77th St./Lexington Av.
Good Turkish cuisine at very low prices.

J. G. MELON'S 340 Amst'dam Av at 76th St.; 1291 Third Av at 74th St.
•Daily till late. Bus M7, M11. S 1 to 79th St./Broadway.
Excellent neighbourhood bars serving American-style food.

O'NEAL'S 48 W 63rd St. opposite Lincoln Center.
•Daily till late. Bus M5, M7, M11, M30, M104. S 1 to Lincoln Center.
Attractive bar offering good beer and hamburgers.

PATSY'S PIZZA 2287 First Av between 117th St. & 118th St.
•Daily till late. Bus M20, M101, M102. S 4, 6 to 116th St./Lexington Av.
The place to come for a pizza in Harlem (see CITY DISTRICTS, A-Z).

SYLVIA'S RESTAURANT 328 Lenox Av between 126th St. & 127th St.
•Daily. Bus M7, M102. S 2, 3 to 125th St./Lenox Av.
The best soul food in NYC. Huge portions at low prices.

POPOVER CAFÉ 551 Amsterdam Av at 87th St.
•0830-2300 Mon.-Fri., 1000-2300 Sat., 1000-2200 Sun. Bus M7, M11. S 1 to 86th St./Broadway.
Huge American breakfasts and brunches to last you through the day.

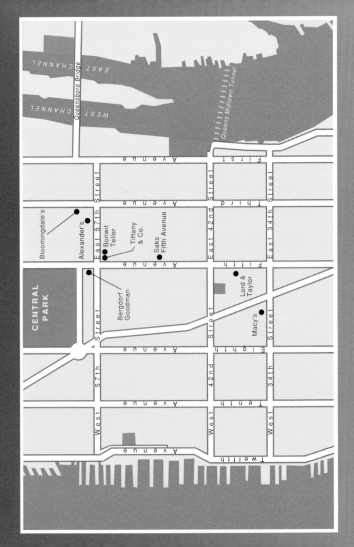

Stores

See **Opening Times**, **Shopping**.

ALEXANDER'S 731 Lexington Av at E 59th St.
Bus M101, M102. S N, R, 4-6 to 59th St./Lexington Av.
Popular treasure-house of bargains.

BERGDORF GOODMAN 754 Fifth Av between W 57th St. & W 58th St.
Bus M1-M5, M32. S N, R to Fifth Av/59th St./60th St.
Shopping on a grand scale. Carries a large range of fashion collections.

BLOOMINGDALE'S 1000 Third Av at 59th St.
Bus M101-M103. S N, R, 4-6 to Lexington Av/59th St.
The quintessential New York City department store.

BONWIT TELLER Trump Tower, 4 E 57th St.
Bus M1-M5, M32. S N, R to Fifth Av/59th/60th St.
Quality high-fashion clothes and accessories for men and women.

LORD & TAYLOR 424 Fifth Av between 38th St. & 39th St.
Bus M1-M5. S B, D, F to 42nd St.
Long-established store selling classic American fashions and accessories, household items and antique furniture. Good for browsing.

MACY'S 151 W 34th St.
Bus M4-M7, M16. S B, D, F, N, R to 34th St.
The world's largest department store has absolutely everything for everyone.

SAKS FIFTH AVENUE 611 Fifth Av at 50th St.
Bus M1-M5, M32. S E, F to Fifth Av/53rd St.
Sophisticated, elegant clothing from top American and European designers.

TIFFANY & CO. 727 Fifth Av at 57th St.
Bus M1-M5, M32. S N, R to Fifth Av/59th St./60th St.
The one and only Tiffany's, selling jewellery, silverware and, surprisingly, some less expensive gift items.

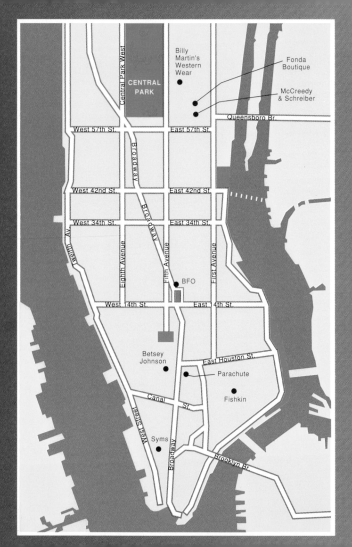

Clothes

BETSEY JOHNSON 130 Thompson St. between Prince St. & Houston St.
Bus M1, M5, M6, M21. S A, E, K to Spring St./Sixth Av.
The latest women's fashions in this designer's own store.

BILLY MARTIN'S WESTERN WEAR 812 Madison at 68th St.
Bus M1-M4, M30. S 6 to 68th St./Hunter College/Lexington Av.
Expensive dude-ranch outfitters. Western clothing for men and women.

FONDA BOUTIQUE 209 E 60th St.
Bus M15, M101, M102. S N, R to 60th St.; 4, 5 to 59th St.
The place to come for women's clothing that is both extremely up-to-date and a little out-of-the-ordinary.

McCREEDY & SCHREIBER 213 E 59th St.
Bus M32, M98, M101, M102, M103. S B, N, R to 60th St.
Every imaginable type of footwear for men, and all at reasonable prices.

PARACHUTE 121 Wooster St. at Spring St.
Bus M6, M12. S C, E to Spring St.
Ultra-modern women's fashions. Not cheap, but great fun (although the staff and the regulars take it all very seriously).

BFO 149 Fifth Av at 21st St.
Bus M2, M3, M5. S N, R to 23rd St./Broadway.
Best names in menswear at the best prices (more than 50% cheaper than department stores).

SYMS 45 Park Pl between Church St. & W Broadway.
Bus M1, M6, M15, M22, M101, M102. S 2, 3 to Park Pl; A, C, 1, 2 to Chambers St.; E to World Trade Center.
Bargain clothing for all the family. Low prices for up-market names.

FISHKIN 314 Grand St. near Allan St.
Bus M8, M15. S B, D to Grand St.
Another establishment selling high-quality goods at keen prices.

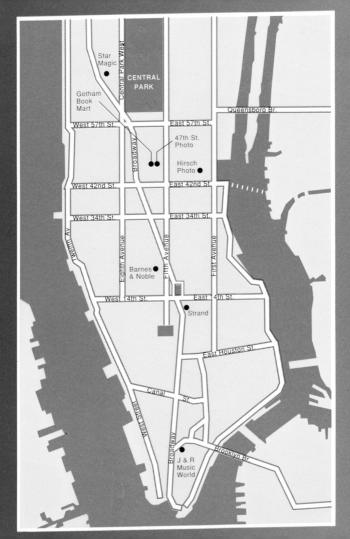

Miscellaneous

BARNES & NOBLE 105 Fifth Av at 18th St.
•0930-2100 Mon.-Fri., 0930-1900 Sat., 1100-1800 Sun.
Bus M2, M3, M5. S L, N, R, 4-6 to Union Sq.
The world's largest bookstore. The Sale Annex across the street (at 128 Fifth Av) has thousands of discounted books on offer.

47TH ST. PHOTO 67 W 47th St. between Fifth Av & Sixth Av.
•0900-1800 Mon.-Thurs., 0900-1400 Fri., 1000-1600 Sun.
Bus M5-M7. S B, D, F to 47th St./50th St./Rockefeller Center.
You need to know what you want in this electrical goods store! The staff may be too busy to be much help, but the prices are good.

HIRSCH PHOTO 699 Third Av at 44th St.
•0800-1800 Mon.-Fri., 1000-1530 Sat. Bus M101, M102. S S, 4-7 to Grand Central Station.
Helpful staff and good deals on second-hand cameras.

J & R MUSIC WORLD 23 Park Row between Ann St. & Beekman St.
•0930-1830 Mon.-Sat. Bus M1, M6, M15, M22, M101. S 4-6 to Brooklyn Bridge.
The latest releases at reasonable prices. Few independent labels or imports.

GOTHAM BOOK MART 41 W 47th St. between Fifth Av & Sixth Av.
•0930-1830 Mon.-Fri., 0930-1800 Sat. Bus M5-M7. S B, D, F to 47th St./50th St./Rockefeller Center.
Crammed full of new and second-hand books. Good film and poetry sections.

STAR MAGIC 275 Amsterdam Av at 73rd St.
•1000-1730. Bus M5, M7, M11, M30, M103, M 108. S 1, 2 to 72nd St./Broadway.
Everything astral and New Age - telescopes, crystals, hologram jewellery.

STRAND 828 Broadway at 12th St.
•0930-2130 Mon.-Fri., 0930-1825 Sat., 1100-1700 Sun. Bus M6, M7. S L, N, R, 4-6 to Union Sq/14th St.
The best second-hand book store in NYC - wonderful bargains.

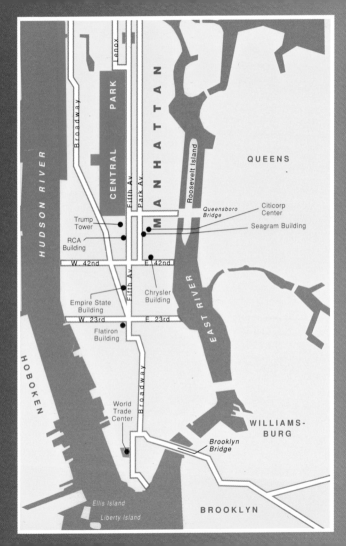

CHRYSLER BUILDING Lexington Av at 42nd St.
Bus M1-M4, M32. S S, 4-7 to Grand Central.
Spectacular Art Deco skyscraper. See **WALK 3**, **A-Z**.

CITICORP CENTER Lexington Av at 53rd St.
Bus M101, M102. S E, F to 53rd St./Lexington Av; 6 to 51st St.
NYC's fifth tallest building. Distinctive slanted roof and an atrium. See **A-Z**.

EMPIRE STATE BUILDING Fifth Av at 34th St.
Bus M1-M5. S B, D, F, S to 34th St./Herald Sq; 6 to 33rd St./Park Av.
Art Deco masterpiece. Observation areas on floors 86 and 102. See **A-Z**.

RCA BUILDING 30 Rockefeller Plaza between 49th St. & 50th St.
Bus M5-M7. S B, D, F to Rockefeller Center.
Home of NBC studios and Radio City Music Hall. Rooftop observation platform (1000-2100 Apr.-Sept.; 1100-1900 Oct.-Mar.). See **Rockefeller Center**.

SEAGRAM BUILDING 375 Park Av between 52nd St. & 53rd St.
Bus M1-M4, M32, M101, M102. S E, F to 53rd St./ Lexington Av,
61st St./Lexington Av.
Bronze and glass building by Philip Johnson and Mies Van der Rohe. See **A-Z**.

TRUMP TOWER 725 Fifth Av at 57th St.
Bus M1-M4, M28, M30, M32. S 4-6 to 59th St./Lexington Av; N, R to
Fifth Av/60th St.
Spectacular building. Extravagant atrium housing exclusive shops. See **A-Z**.

WORLD TRADE CENTER World Trade Center Plaza on Church St.
Bus M1, M6, M10, M22. S A, C, E, K, 2, 3 to World Trade Center.
Twin towers dominating the city. No. 2 boasts the highest open-air observation deck in the world (closed in bad weather; $2.95, child $1.50). See **A-Z**.

FLATIRON BUILDING Fifth Av. & Broadway.
Bus M2, M3, M5, M26, M32. S N, R to 23rd St.
Built in 1902, this wedge-shaped landmark was one of the earliest buildings to be constructed with a steel frame. See **Madison Square**.

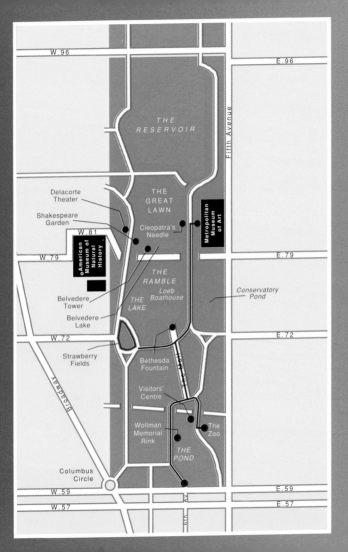

Central Park

1 hr 30 min - excluding boating trips, visits to galleries, etc.
While the park is generally safe during daylight hours you should avoid straying from the main thoroughfares.

Begin at the entrance to the park on 59th St. and Sixth Av. Follow the avenue into the park where it veers to the left, passing the Pond, on your right, and continuing past the Wollman Memorial Rink. Turn right towards East Dr and call in at the Dairy, now a Visitors' Center, where you can obtain maps and information. Once on East Dr turn left to reach the zoo (see **Zoos**) - the Children's Zoo is just north of the main zoo. Next, turn right up East Dr to the Mall, a long, tree-lined path leading to the beautiful Bethesda Fountain and, just beyond that, the Lake. Turn left before the fountain and walk towards the Dakota Building (see **A-Z**) on 72nd St., across from which is Strawberry Fields, the two-and-a-half-acre memorial to John Lennon, planted with many trees, shrubs and flowers sent as gifts of peace from other countries. Return to the fountain and take a left turn up to the Loeb Boathouse where there are rowing boats and bicycles for hire (see **Bicycle and Motorbike Hire**). East of the Lake and Boathouse is the Conservatory Pond, with statues of Alice in Wonderland and Hans Christian Andersen, where the young, and young-at-heart, sail model yachts. Children's storytelling sessions are held here during the summer (Wed., Sat.) and you can hire rowing boats. Walking northwards on East Dr you will see the Ramble to the left just beyond the Lake, a wooded hill criss-crossed by little paths much favoured by bird-watchers and muggers. Avoid going in! Carry on along the same route past Belvedere Lake. The 'medieval' Belvedere Tower stands to the south west of the lake across from the Ramble and overlooks the north side of the park. (The Shakespeare Garden is just west of it, and the Delacorte Theater - see **Theatre** - is to the north.) Continuing in the same direction you soon come to Cleopatra's Needle. The Great Lawn beyond is much used for games. The Metropolitan Museum of Art (see **ART GALLERIES**, **A-Z**) stands on the right. There is little of interest beyond here other than the Reservoir, beloved of joggers, and the Conservatory Garden. Relax in the Met's café, on the south side of the building, before leaving the park by the 72nd St. exit. See **CITY SIGHTS**, **PARKS**, **Central Park**.

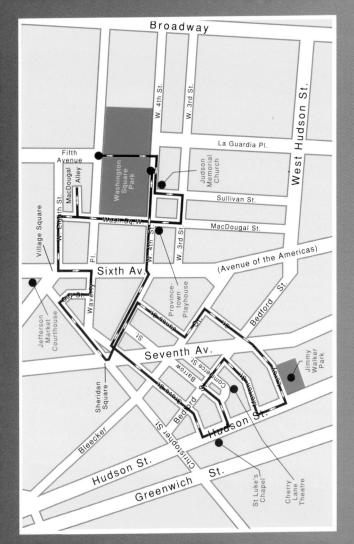

Greenwich Village

30 min-1 hr

Start at Washington Square Arch (see **A-Z**) at the beginning of Fifth Av. Cross to the south side of the park, but look back as you go to see the handsome buildings bordering its northern side. Turn right as you leave the park and you will see the Judson Memorial Church on your left. Turn left into Sullivan St., then right into W Third St., and then right again into MacDougal St., passing the Provincetown Playhouse on your left. Continue along MacDougal St., as it becomes Washington Square West and then MacDougal St. again, before turning right into MacDougal Alley to see the little mews belonging to the houses on the square, which were formerly stables. Return to MacDougal St. and turn left onto W Eighth St. (lined with shoe shops), heading towards Sixth Av, until you arrive at the Village Square dominated by the Jefferson Market Courthouse (now a library).

Turn left onto Sixth Av, right into Waverly Pl and then right again into Gay St. Turn left onto Christopher St. and walk past Waverly Pl to Sheridan Sq at Seventh Av. Turn left into W Fourth St. and stroll past the shops and cafés to Jones St. Follow Jones St., turn left onto Bleecker St., then right onto Leroy St. Continue along Leroy St. across Seventh Av to St Luke's Pl and the Jimmy Walker Park which commemorates a flamboyant jazz age mayor of New York who lived at No. 6 St Luke's Pl (Theodore Dreiser wrote *An American Tragedy* at No. 16).

Turn right into Hudson St. and right again into Morton St. which brings you to Bedford St. Edna St Vincent Millay and John Barrymore are thought to have lived at No. 75 1/2, reputedly the narrowest house in New York City. (Take a detour onto Commerce St. to see other wooden houses and an old barn, at No. 38, which is the home of the Cherry Lane Theater.)

A left turn onto Barrow St. and then a right onto Hudson St. brings you to St Luke's Chapel. Turn right from here into Grove St., a peaceful area contrasting sharply with the bustle of Bleecker St., and continue along it to W Fourth St., passing Grove Court on the right. Follow W Fourth St. across Sixth Av and back to Washington Sq (see **A-Z**). See **CITY DISTRICTS**, **Greenwich Village**.

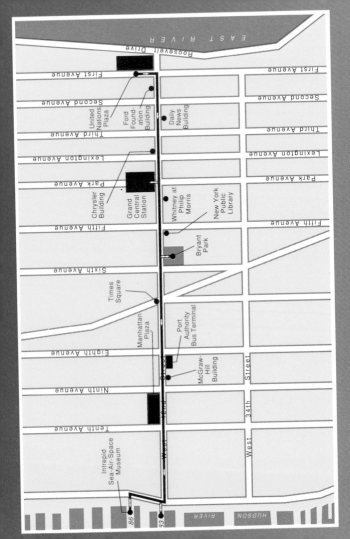

42nd Street

1 hr Start at the UN Plaza outside the United Nations Headquarters (see **CITY SIGHTS**, **A-Z**) on First Av and turn onto 42nd St. Head due west along the street until you reach the Ford Foundation Building (see **A-Z**), on the right, which has the finest indoor atrium in the city. Continuing on in the same direction you come to the Daily News Building (see **A-Z**), on the left-hand side of 42nd St., where *Superman* was filmed. Your next stop should be at the junction with Lexington Av, where you can admire the splendid Art Deco Chrysler Building (see **SKYSCRAPERS**, **A-Z**). The Grand Hyatt Hotel and then Grand Central Station (see **A-Z**) are just a little further on. This part of 42nd st. street has many fine Beaux Arts buildings, such as the Bowery Savings Bank across from the station, which have elaborately decorated lobbies you can pop in and visit. The Whitney at Philip Morris across the street is one of the three other galleries which exhibits the works of the Whitney Museum of American Art (see **ART GALLERIES**, **A-Z**). It includes a small Picture Gallery and a Sculpture Court. Further along, at the corner of Fifth Av, is the New York Public Library (see **A-Z**). Bryant Park (see **PARKS**, **A-Z**), containing second-hand book stalls and a TKTS booth for music and dance events (see **Theatre**), is just past the library on the same side of the street.

Continue west to Times Sq (see **CITY SIGHTS**, **A-Z**) and enjoy the sight of one of the busiest and most famous crossroads in the world. There is a branch of the New York Convention and Visitors Bureau (see **Tourist Information**) where you can obtain sightseeing information and 'twofer' theatre vouchers, and, on the north side of the square, the TKTS booth selling discounted theatre tickets (see **Theatre**).

Keep going past the pornography theatres (between Seventh Av and Eighth Av) and the Port Authority Bus Terminal (see **Buses**). Note the old McGraw-Hill Building on your left, a bit further on, which has been designated a City Landmark. The Holy Cross church opposite is the oldest building on 42nd St. (there is a statue at the north side of Times Sq of its former pastor, Father Duffy).

If you have time, take a detour along Ninth Av into the area of Paddy's Market (between 38th St. and 44th St.), which is no longer a true market, but contains a wealth of different food shops. This is the site of the Ninth Avenue International Festival held in May (see **Events**).

Returning to the stretch of 42nd St. between Ninth Av and Tenth Av you come to Theater Row, housing many off-Broadway theatres, and Manhattan Plaza, the residence of artists and actors.

Continue to the end of 42nd St. and turn up 12th Av to the end of 43rd St. where you can reach Pier 83, the departure point for a Circle Line cruise (see **Ferries**) round the island of Manhattan. Turn northwards up 12th Av from here to Pier 86, site of the *Intrepid* Sea-Air-Space Museum, an aircraft carrier displaying fighter planes, prototype models and other paraphernalia of war.

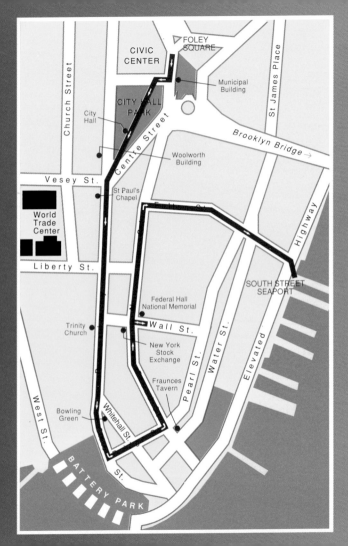

Heritage Trail

30 min-1 hr A three-mile walk following The Heritage Trail. A map of the trail, pinpointing the 17 heritage landmarks, can be obtained from the New York Convention and Visitors Bureau (see **Tourist Information***). Take the No. 6 train to Brooklyn Bridge Station.*

Start at Foley Sq in the Civic Center (see **A-Z**) and walk south to the Municipal Building (crowned by the statue of *Civic Fame*) at No. 1 Centre St. Cross over Centre St., and walk past City Hall and through City Hall Park to Broadway (see **A-Z**). Continue down Broadway to the Woolworth Building (see **A-Z**) and admire the humorous caricatures of the owner, architect and builder in the lobby. Keep heading south along Broadway past St Paul's Chapel (see **CHURCHES**, **A-Z**) and Trinity Church (see **CHURCHES**, **A-Z**) until you reach the Bowling Green (see **A-Z**). Battery Park (see **PARKS**, **A-Z**) across the road contains Castle Clinton (see **A-Z**) which faces out towards the harbour.

Keep going along the adjoining State St. and then turn left along Bridge St. to the Fraunces Tavern (see **A-Z**) at the corner of Pearl St. and Broad St. It contains a Museum of the Revolutionary War as well as a restaurant which serves excellent breakfasts. Turn onto Broad St., going in a northerly direction, and follow it to Wall St. where you can visit the New York Stock Exchange (see **A-Z**). Continue north on Broad St. again, past the Federal Hall National Memorial (see **A-Z**), and then keep going in the same direction along the adjoining Nassau St. to the Federal Reserve Bank at Liberty St. Continue on until you reach Fulton St., then turn right into it and head for the East River. You are now in the heart of the South Street Seaport (see **CITY SIGHTS**, **A-Z**).

Accidents and Breakdowns: In the event of an accident follow the usual procedure of exchanging names, addresses and insurance details. To contact the police or other emergency services, tel: 911 (see **Emergency Numbers**). If someone is injured and you are held responsible, insist on contacting your embassy or consulate (see **A-Z**) as soon as possible.

In the case of breakdowns contact the American Automobile Association (AAA) at 28 E 78th St., and Broadway at 62nd St., which offers an emergency road service to members (tel: 212-757-3356), or phone the nearest garage. Call 594-0700 for a report on road conditions before you set out. See **Car Hire**, **Driving**.

Accommodation: There are 100,000 hotel rooms in more than 1000 hotels in New York City which range in price from $30, in the no-frills YMCA, to $300 in the luxurious Waldorf Towers. The average

price for a room for one night is $100 (without breakfast). You should expect to pay the following in the various categories:

De luxe	over $200.
Luxury	$125-$200.
Moderate	$85-$125.
Budget	$70-$85.
No Frills	under $70.

In addition, there is a 5% tax on hotel rooms, plus a sales tax of 8.25% and a bed tax of $2 per person.

It is advisable to make hotel reservations in advance of visiting the city, especially in spring and autumn when the hotels are filled with convention delegates. If you do arrive without a reservation Meegan Hotel Reservation Service at JFK International Airport (see **Airports**) provides a booking service for a wide range of hotels (tel: 718-995-9292/800-221-1235). Although the New York Convention and Visitors Bureau (see **Tourist Information**) does not provide this service, it can issue you with a list of hotels with their price ranges and telephone numbers (0900-1800 Mon.-Fri.).

The following types of accommodation are also recommended:
Women only - Martha Washington, 30 E 30th St., tel: 689-1900; Allerton House, 130 E 57th St., tel: 753-8841.

Manhattan East Suite Hotels - Nine branches throughout Manhattan, tel: 1-800-637-8433 for locations and prices. Suites with kitchenettes for the price of most luxury hotel rooms.

Bed and breakfast - Urban Ventures, 306 W 38th St., tel: 594-5650; City Lights Bed & Breakfast, 308 E 79th St., tel: 737-7049; New World Bed & Breakfast, 150 Fifth Av, tel: 675-5600. See **Camping and Caravanning**.

Airports: New York City is served by three major airports:
John F. Kennedy International (JFK) - 24 km from midtown Manhattan in south-east Queens. Handles international flights. Transport to and from the airport includes the Carey Bus (see **Buses**) which departs every 20 min for Grand Central Station and the Port Authority Terminal in midtown Manhattan (takes 1 hr; $8); the JFK 'Train to the Plane' Express combining bus and subway travel ($6.50); and a free shuttle bus con-

necting all the airline terminals to the subway system (only recommended if you have few items of luggage). The subway takes about 75 min to reach Manhattan. Taxis (see **A-Z**) are the easiest means of transportation to and from all the airports (approximately $30 from JFK).

Newark International (EWR) - 25.6 km from midtown Manhattan in north-east New Jersey. Handles international flights. Olympia Trails and NJ (New Jersey) Transit provide bus transport into Manhattan (takes 40 min; $7). The taxi fare is $40.

La Guardia (LGA) - 12.8 km from midtown Manhattan in north-west Queens. Handles internal flights. Connections to Manhattan include the Carey Bus (see **Buses**) to Grand Central Station and Port Authority Terminal (takes 30 min; $6); the Pan Am water-shuttle service (tel: 212-797-9485 for a timetable) from Pier 11 at the end of Wall St. to Marine Air Terminal (takes approximately 30 min; $20). The taxi fare is $20. There are no tourist offices at the airports (see **Tourist Information**). Dial 800-AIR-RIDE (see **Telephones and Telegrams**) for further information on transport to and from the airports.

American Museum of Natural History: Don't miss the display of dinosaur fossils for which the museum is most famous. Other attractions include the Hall of Meteorites, which houses the *Star of India*, the largest blue sapphire in the world (563 carats), and the Hall of Ocean Life containing a 94-ft suspended replica of a blue whale. The Hall of African Mammals on the second floor is home to dioramas of elephants, lions, zebras, giraffes, etc, while the third floor has the Naturemax Theater, with the largest indoor screen in New York (four storeys high) which shows documentaries. The Hayden Planetarium is adjacent to the museum (see CHILDREN, **A-Z**). See CHILDREN.

Art Galleries: In addition to all the public galleries in NYC, there are 400 private galleries along Madison Av (in the high 60s and 70s) and 57th St., plus those in SoHo (see CITY DISTRICTS, **A-Z**) and the East Village (see CITY DISTRICTS, **A-Z**). See ART GALLERIES.

Astors: Along with the Rockefellers (see **A-Z**) and the Vanderbilts (see **A-Z**), the Astors are famous as one of the richest and most powerful families in New York. The founding member was John Jacob Astor, a German immigrant who made his fortune in the fur trade.

Audubon Terrace: A fine terrace situated at 155th St. and Broadway, which is home to several museums, including the Museum of the American Indian (see MUSEUMS 1) and the Hispanic Museum (see MUSEUMS 2).

Avenue of the Americas: The official name for Sixth Av. Most New Yorkers refer to it as Sixth Av, and we follow their example when quoting it in the addresses and directions in this book.

Baby-sitting: Part Time Child Care, 19 E 69th St. (tel: 879-4343); Avalon Registry, 116 Central Park South (tel: 245-0250).
Contact the Babysitters Guild, 60 E 42nd St. (tel: 682-0227), or the Babysitters Association, 610 Cathedral Parkway (tel: 865-9348), for a list of more agencies or for guidance.
There are day-care facilities at the Children's All Day School, 109 E 60th St. (tel: 752-4566); the Multimedia Pre-school, 40 Sutton Pl at 59th St. (tel: 593-1041); and the Children's Workshop, 17 E 16th St. off Fifth Av (tel: 691-8964). There is also a crèche at the Children's Museum of Manhattan, 314 W 54th St. (tel: 765-5904).

Banks: See Money.

Battery Park: Lies at the tip of Manhattan (see A-Z) and offers good views of the harbour. The ferry terminals (see **Ferries**) for all the islands are situated here, including the Staten Island Ferry (see CITY SIGHTS, A-Z). The Battery was used to defend the island of Manhattan against the British. See PARKS, WALK 4.

Best Buys: Things to look out for are fashions, jewellery, linens, china, records and tapes. Keep an eye out for sales where you can pick up goods at discount prices. New York is also the most price-competitive city in the US for camera, video and electronic equipment. See SHOPPING, **Markets**, **Shopping**.

Bicycle and Motorbike Hire: It is possible to hire bicycles in Central Park (see **CITY SIGHTS**, **PARKS**, **WALK 1**, **A-Z**) at Andy's Bicycles in the Park, 72nd St. and the Loeb Boathouse (see **WALK 1**). In Manhattan (see **A-Z**) you can also hire them from West Side Bicycles, 231 W 96th St. at Broadway; Pedal Pusher, 1306 Second Av between 68th St. and 69th St.; Midtown Bicycles, 360 W 47th St. at Ninth Av; and Sixth Av Bicycles, 546 Sixth Av at 15th St. However, riding a bike in the city can be dangerous, nor is it recommended for visitors to Central Park. If you must hire one you have to be able to produce ID. The cost is approximately $4 per hour, deposit required.

Botanical Gardens: *New York Botanical Garden* - an indoor/outdoor 250-acre paradise, just north of the Bronx Zoo (see **CHILDREN**, **Zoos**), containing a Rose Garden, a Herb Garden, a Rock Garden and a Native Plant Garden (open daily; free). You can reach it on Metro-North from Grand Central Station.
Brooklyn Botanic Garden - attractive gardens, adjoining the Brooklyn Museum (see **ART GALLERIES**) at 1000 Washington Av, which include a Japanese Hill, a Pond Garden, a Shakespeare Garden and a Fragrance Garden for the Blind. See **PARKS**.

Bowery: This street, named after *bouwerie* (the Dutch for 'farm'), stretches from Canal Street, just above Chinatown (see **CITY DISTRICTS**, **A-Z**), east of Little Italy (see **CITY DISTRICTS**, **A-Z**) and Greenwich Village (see **CITY DISTRICTS**, **A-Z**) to Cooper Square. Its notoriety goes back to its vaudeville days when the 'Bowery Boys' robbed the patrons of dance halls and bars. The area now has a large vagrant population. Look out for the Savings Bank at No. 130 which makes a definite architectural statement about the nature of financial security.

Bowling Green: This area at the end of Broadway has been a bowling green, a cattle market and a parade ground in its time. It is also the legendary spot where Peter Minuit traded $24 worth of trinkets to the Indians for the rights to Manhattan (see **A-Z**). The building behind the green is the old Customs House which is decorated with sculptures of the continents of Europe, Africa, Asia and America. See **WALK 4**.

Broadway: The USA's longest street, stretching 146 miles to Albany. This is New York's Theater District (see **CITY DISTRICTS**), at the heart of which lies Times Square (see **CITY SIGHTS**, **A-Z**). See **WALK 4**.

Bronx, The: This borough to the north of Manhattan (see **A-Z**) across the Harlem River, contains the Bronx Zoo (see **CHILDREN**, **ZOOS**), the Edgar Allan Poe Cottage, the New York Botanical Garden (see **Botanical Gardens**), City Island (which looks like a coastal fishing village) and Belmont. There is also an Italian market on Arthur Avenue.

Brooklyn: Although in the process of becoming 'yuppified', this borough has a lot to offer visitors to New York. There is the Brooklyn Academy of Music (see **MUSIC VENUES**, **A-Z**), the Brooklyn Children's Museum (see **CHILDREN**), the Brooklyn Museum (see **ART GALLERIES**) in Prospect Park (see **PARKS**) and Coney Island (see **A-Z**). A walk across the magnificent Brooklyn Bridge (see **A-Z**) brings you to the fashionable district of Brooklyn Heights, full of old American houses. From here the subway will take you to other parts such as Carroll Gardens, Cobble Hill and Prospect Park (avoid Bedford-Stuyvesant, a notorious ghetto). Brooklyn has the largest population of the five boroughs.

Brooklyn Academy of Music (BAM): This world famous academy stages a Next Wave Festival of avant-garde performances in dance and music every autumn. In the spring there is a Black Dance Festival featuring diverse forms of music and movement. See **MUSIC VENUES**.

Brooklyn Bridge: This was New York City's first suspension bridge. The best way to see the bridge is to take subways A, E to High St./Brooklyn Bridge and to walk back across it along the pedestrian deck above the road to Manhattan (see **A-Z**). See **Brooklyn**.

Bryant Park: This park behind the New York Public Library is named after William Cullen Bryant, the editor of the *New York Post* who campaigned for Central Park (see **CITY SIGHTS, PARKS, WALK 1, A-Z**) when the site it now occupies was a swamp. See **PARKS, WALK 3**.

Budget:

Discos	$20 admission, $5 per drink.
Broadway show	$25-$50.
Off-Broadway show	$8-$35.
Cinemas	$6-$7.
Museums	$2-$5 (some ask for donations only, many are free on Tuesday evenings).
Breakfast	$3 (local coffee shop), $8 (hotel).
Lunch	$4 (sandwich and drink).

Buses: City buses (MTA) have blue numbers (preceded by the letter M) and display a list of the streets through which they pass (in red). They require an exact fare of $1 in coins or tokens (purchased from subway token booths). Place your fare in the box at the front of the bus upon entering and if taking an intersecting route ask for a free transfer (if you are not sure ask the driver). There are no tourist or weekly passes. The service runs 24 hr, but is less frequent late at night. The buses are punctual, clean and comfortable, but slow.

The city's main Port Authority Bus Terminal (see **WALK 3**), at 40th St. and Eighth Av, has three tiers of shops, eateries and bus platforms with connections to destinations all over the US. You can also catch the NJ

Transit buses to Newark Airport and the Carey buses to JFK and La Guardia Airports at the Air Transcenter here (see **Airports**). Many weirdos, drug addicts and winos hang about this area so carry your own baggage and hail your own taxi. You can reach the terminal on subways A, C, E , K or buses M10, M42, M106. See **Smoking**.

Cameras and Photography: A wide variety of photographic equipment is available in the city, especially in the area around the west 30s and 40s which has a huge selection of camera stores. Films, batteries and VHS (NTSC) tapes are also sold in drugstores, electronics shops and some delis. Nikon House, 620 Fifth Av at 50th St., has a free photo gallery and repair centre, holds seminars on photography, gives out free information on cameras and rents out equipment (tel: 586-3907). See **SHOPPING 3**, **Best Buys**.

Camping and Caravanning: There are no camp sites in New York City itself, but on Long Island (see **A-Z**) there are the Old Bethpage, at Claremont Road and East Islip, and the Heckscher State Park, tel: 516-794-4222. Call 212-309-0560 to obtain a free 'I Love New York' camping map of New York State. Caravans can be parked in New Jersey at the New Yorker Trailer City, West New York, tel: NJ 201-866-0999.

Car Hire: Driving in New York City is most definitely not recommended. If you want to hire a car for touring outside the city you must be 25 years of age, and have a major credit card and valid driving licence (foreign licences accepted). Collision damage waiver and personal injury insurance are advisable. The names and addresses of hire firms are listed in the Yellow Pages. Look out for special weekend and weekly rates advertised in newspapers. The cost of hiring a car is approximately $50 per day. See **Accidents and Breakdowns**, **Driving**.

Carnegie Hall: This grand concert hall, seating 2800 people, was built in 1883 with help from the famous Scottish-American industrialist Andrew Carnegie. The hall was almost demolished after the Lincoln Center (see **MUSIC VENUES**, **A-Z**) opened but its acoustics have been improved and the hall is now a preserved building. See **MUSIC VENUES**.

Cast-Iron Buildings: These were built in the period from the 1850s to the 1890s when it was discovered that it was easier to construct buildings of cast iron, thin iron columns being capable of bearing as much weight as thick stone walls. Elaborate decoration was already a feature of stonework and again it was found to be easier and cheaper to employ it in the moulding of cast iron. The best of the cast-iron buildings are situated on Greene Street in SoHo (see CITY DISTRICTS, **A-Z**).

Castle Clinton: This fort was originally sited out in the harbour in order to provide crossfire for the Battery which gave Battery Park (see PARKS, **A-Z**) its name. The stretch of water between them was filled in and now the castle is in Battery Park itself. Prior to its restoration as a fort, and its designation as a national monument, it served as a concert venue, an immigration centre and an aquarium. See WALK 4.

Cathedral of St John the Divine: See St John the Divine.

Central Park: New Yorkers owe the existence of Central Park to the campaigning of William Cullen Bryant (see **Bryant Park**) and the architectural genius of Frederick Law Olmsted (see **A-Z**) and Calvert Vaux. Nearly 20% of the park's area consists of water and you can visit a model-boat pond, go out on the Lake in a rowing boat - or even in a Venetian gondola. For theatre buffs, there is the Delacorte Theater which hosts the free 'Shakespeare in the Park' festival during the sum-

mer (see **Events**, **Theatre**). Other attractions include a newly-redesigned zoo (see **Zoos**), ice-skating rinks, horse-riding trails, jogging routes, hansom-cab rides and bird-watching tours (organized, April-June, by the NYC Audubon Society, 950 Third Av, tel: 832-3200). See **CITY SIGHTS**, **PARKS**, **WALK 1**.

Chelsea: This area, stretching from 14th St. to 34th St. and from the Sixth Av to the Hudson River, has little of interest for the visitor apart from the Chelsea Hotel (see **A-Z**). It is mostly a residential district, but has an array of bars and restaurants along Eighth Av. You can reach it on buses M5, M6, M10, M11 and subways A-C, E, F, K, S to 23rd St.

Chelsea Hotel: The hotel's literary associations began when Chelsea (see **A-Z**) was New York's theatre district. Some famous writers and artists, such as Mark Twain, Tennessee Williams, Brendan Behan, Bob Dylan and Andy Warhol, have lived and worked in this Gothic pile at 222 W 23rd St., with its wrought-iron balconies and its elaborate staircase.

Chemists: Kaufman Pharmacy at 50th St. and Lexington Av is open 24 hr, tel: 755-2266.

Children: In addition to the attractions listed in the 'topics' section of this book (see **CHILDREN**, **CITY SIGHTS**) there are special children's activities available throughout the five boroughs which you can check for in the local press (see **What's On**). But if in doubt, head for the area of Central Park stretching from Fifth Av to Central Park West and 59th St. to 110th St., where there is a zoo, a carousel, a puppet theatre, rowing boats for hire, horse-riding and roller skating (see **CITY SIGHTS**, **PARKS**, **WALK 1**, **Central Park**).

To find out about sports for children contact the YMCA's West Side Branch at 5 W 63rd St. (tel: 787-4400) or its Vanderbilt Branch at 224 E 47th St. (tel: 755-2410). As for quieter pursuits, there are children's libraries in the Jefferson Market Library at 425 Sixth Av and the New York Public Library (see **WALK 3**, **A-Z**) at 42nd St. and Fifth Av. There is also the Donnell Library Children's Room at 20 W 53rd St.

Chinatown: A small but ever-growing area. To the south is the Civic Center (see **WALK 4, A-Z**); the Bowery (see **A-Z**) is to the east; Centre Street to the west. Only to the south has expansion been halted. Most people visit the area in search of cheap food as there are well over 100 restaurants to choose from, and as many food shops. See **CITY DISTRICTS**.

Chrysler Building: For a short time, before the Empire State Building was completed, this was New York's tallest building and many feel that, with its Art Deco crown, it is still the city's finest. The architecture is based on car designs from the 1920s. The opulent lobby is the only part of the building open to the public. See **SKYSCRAPERS, WALK 3**.

Cigarettes and Tobacco: Cigarettes are sold in vending machines in bars and restaurants, in delis, drugstores, supermarkets and at newsstands. See **Smoking**.

Cinemas: Tickets for a first-run film must be purchased at least an hour before the film begins. Ticket holders then queue in front of the cinema for the best seats. In addition to the usual mixture of first-runs, cult films and golden oldies shown in the cinemas, there are special screenings by the Museum of Modern Art (see **ART GALLERIES, A-Z**), the

American Museum of Natural History (see **CHILDREN**, **A-Z**) and the Alliance Francaise, 22 E 60th St. See **Budget**, **What's On**.

Citicorp Center: The Center's steeply-angled roof was intended to provide solar power for the building, but unfortunately it doesn't work. The three-storey atrium, decorated with tumbling greenery, houses an excellent shopping area with restaurants. The little Lutheran church of St Peter's (see **CHURCHES**) has a chapel where you can attend jazz concerts (1230 Wed.) and jazz vespers (1700 Sun.). See **SKYSCRAPERS**.

Civic Center: Situated in City Hall Park, the Civic Center comprises City Hall, a beautiful New York City landmark housing the Mayor's office and historic exhibits, the Woolworth Building, facing City Hall, and the Tweed Courthouse, behind it, which is named after the notorious NYC boss who ran the city for his own gain. See **WALK 4**.

Climate: Spring is usually mild, but can sometimes be unpredictable and rainy (average 10°C). Autumn is normally clear, sharp and short-lived (average 14°C). The winter months, from November to March, are cold (average 4°C) while summer can be extremely hot and humid (average 23°C). Tel: 976-1212 for recorded weather reports.

Cloisters: This is the medieval collection of the Metropolitan Museum of Art (see **ART GALLERIES**, **WALK 1**, **A-Z**). Exhibited in a dramatic setting high above the Hudson River (see **A-Z**) at the northern tip of Manhattan (see **A-Z**), it consists of parts of five medieval monasteries transported brick by brick from Europe and reconstructed here as examples of 12th-15thC Gothic architecture. Highlights include a Romanesque chapel, the Unicorn tapestries, stained-glass windows and peaceful gardens with vistas over the Hudson River. See **ART GALLERIES**.

Columbus Circle: Situated at the south-east corner of Central Park (see **CITY SIGHTS**, **PARKS**, **WALK 1**, **A-Z**), where Central Park South crosses Broadway (see **A-Z**) and becomes W 59th St. and Eighth Av becomes Central Park West, this contains a statue of Columbus and the New York Convention and Visitors Bureau (see **Tourist Information**).

Coney Island: Coney Island, off south Brooklyn, is not the place it used to be, but it still has Nathan's, where the hot dog originated, and the Astroland Amusement Park. Other attractions include the New York Aquarium, which has Beluga whales, sea lions, seals, penguins, dolphin shows and a touch-it tank, Brighton and Manhattan beaches and the boardwalk. You can catch subways B, D, F, M, N to Coney Island.

Consulates:
UK - 845 Third Av, tel: 752-5747.
Republic of Ireland - 515 Madison Av, tel: 319-255.
Australia - 636 Fifth Av, tel: 245-4000.
Canada - 1251 Sixth Av, tel: 586-2400.
New Zealand - 630 Fifth Av, tel: 586-0060.

Conversion Charts:

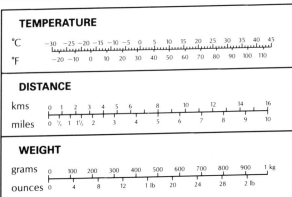

Cooper-Hewitt Museum: Formerly the mansion of the Scottish-American industrialist Andrew Carnegie. It provides an ideal setting for the national design collection of textiles (some as old as 3000 years)

jewellery, furniture, and architectural and design drawings. Lectures, classes, concerts and exhibitions are held here. See **MUSEUMS 1**.

Crime and Theft: In New York City, as in all cities, use your common sense when it comes to protecting yourself and safeguarding your possessions. Don't let anyone carry your luggage for you and always hail your own taxi. You should also try to avoid travelling on the subways at night. Keep valuables in hotel safe deposit boxes.

If you are mugged take a taxi to the nearest precinct (police station) and report the crime immediately (the police will refund the cost of the fare). The police will record the theft and give you a reference number for your insurance company. If you have a credit card or traveller's cheques stolen also contact the company who issued them as soon as possible (see **Money**). See **Emergency Numbers**, **Insurance**.

Culture: Known as the culture capital of the world, New York City has 300 theatres, 150 museums and 400 galleries. Broadway (see **A-Z**) is the hub of the city's cultural activity with its musicals, comedies and dramas. Music and dance range from the traditional to the avant-garde. The New York International Festival of the Arts is a biennial international event with music, dance, theatre and films. See **ART GALLERIES**, **MUSEUMS**, **Cinema**, **Events**, **Museums**, **Theatre**, **What's On**.

Currency: The monetary unit is the dollar ($). There are 100 cents (c) to the dollar. Coins in circulation are valued at one cent (a penny), 5 cents (a nickel), 10 cents (a dime), 25 cents (a quarter) and 50 cents (half a dollar). Banknotes (bills) are in denominations of $1, $5, $10, $20, $50 and $100. There are also $2, $500 and $1000 bills, but they are uncommon. See **Budget**, **Money**, **Traveller's Cheques**.

Customs Chart:

Duty Free Into:	Cigarettes	or	Cigars	or	Tobacco	Spirits	or	Wine
U.S.A.	200		50		3 lbs	1.0 l		1.0 l
U.K.	200		50		250 g	1.0 l		2 l

Daily News Building: This building is probably better known as the offices of *The Globe*, the newspaper which employed Clark Kent and Lois Lane in *Superman*. A globe does actually exist - it is in the lobby, along with clocks displaying the time around the world. See **WALK 3**.

Dakota Building: The name of this building derives from a joke it prompted in 1884 when it was built: that it lay so far north it was actually in Dakota territory. It was the setting for the film *Rosemary's Baby* and the site of John Lennon's assassination in 1980. See **WALK 1**.

Downtown: Anything south of 14th St., the oldest part of Manhattan (see **A-Z**), constitutes downtown. However, in directions, it can also refer to anywhere south of where you are at present. See **Orientation**.

Drinks: The water in NYC is perfectly safe to drink and there is no need to order bottled water unless you prefer it. The selection of alcoholic drinks available in the city is phenomenal, anything from a classic Manhattan cocktail (try one at the Stanhope opposite the Metropolitan Museum of Art - see **ART GALLERIES**, **WALK 1**, **A-Z**) to beer brewed right in Manhattan (see **A-Z**). The better restaurants all offer extensive selections of wine from America (New York State and California), France, Italy, Germany and Australia. There are short tours of New York City's only winery, Schapiro's at 126 Rivington St., on Sundays. See **BARS**.

Driving: Driving is not a good idea in New York City with its vast network of roads and highways, and especially not in Manhattan (see **A-Z**). The headache of traffic jams, especially during rush hours (0800-1000, 1600-1800 Mon.-Fri.) and the expense of parking can be avoided by using public transport (see **Transport**) and taxis (see **A-Z**). Drive on the right-hand side of the road. The speed limit in NYC is 35 mph but that speed is rarely reached. Seat belts are compulsory. If you are caught in an intersection when the light changes your are liable to be given a hefty fine by the traffic police. Right turns through a red light are not permitted and pedestrians have the right of way at crossings. There are tolls on some bridges, but none on the Queensborough, Brooklyn (see **A-Z**), Manhattan, Williamsburg and Willis Av/Third Av Bridges. See **Accidents and Breakdowns**.

Drugs: Expect severe penalties if you are caught buying, selling or using illegal drugs in NYC. See **Emergency Numbers**.

Duffy Square: This square, situated in the north part of Times Square (see **CITY SIGHTS**, **A-Z**) between 46th St. and 47th St., is named after Father Francis P. Duffy, the pastor of Holy Cross Church in 42nd St. (see **WALK 3**). It contains his statue as well as that of George M. Cohan, the song and dance man who wrote *Yankee Doodle Dandy* and

Give My Regards to Broadway. The TKTS ticket booth is also located here (see **Theatre**).

East River: Flowing down from Long Island Sound, the river divides the borough of Queens, on Long Island, from the Bronx on the mainland. Further south, it divides Manhattan from Brooklyn and Queens.

East Village: This district has seen many changes since it was Peter Stuyvesant's estate. The Astors (see **A-Z**) and Vanderbilts (see **A-Z**) lived here in the 19thC before the rising population of eastern European immigrants transformed it into 'Little Ukraine'. In the 1950s the beat poets formed an artists' colony here, and it is now becoming a fashionable district, especially around St Mark's Place. See **CITY DISTRICTS**.

Eating Out: New York has a vast range of different types of restaurants serving foods from every culture imaginable and you are sure to find something to suit both your taste buds and your wallet.
On the streets you have the choice of anything from hot dogs to pretzels, pizzas to ice creams, sodas to *souvlakis*, kebabs to honey-roasted nuts. See **RESTAURANTS**, **Budget**, **Food**.

Ellis Island: Many millions of immigrants passed through the buildings on Ellis Island during its 62 years as the US Immigration Center. It is part of the Statue of Liberty National Monument (see **CITY SIGHTS**, **A-Z**) and is undergoing restoration as a memorial to the different peoples

and cultures who made America (and New York). See **CITY SIGHTS**.

Emergency Numbers:
Police, Fire, Ambulance	911.
Crime Victims Hotline	577-7700.
Medical treatment	683-1010 (E 34th St.).
Missing persons	374-66913.
Police information	347-5000.

Empire State Building: This famous New York landmark has 73 elevators, 6500 windows and a beautiful marble lobby. The building is illuminated in different colours on public holidays (red, white and blue on the 4 July; red and green at Christmas; green on St Patrick's Day - see **Events**). There are wonderful panoramas from the two observation platforms. King Kong's famous visit here with Fay Wray is well-recorded on the souvenirs for sale. The building is open until midnight every day. See **SKYSCRAPERS**.

Equitable Building: It was the building of this massive structure on Broadway (at No. 120) in 1915 that forced the city authorities to restrict the floor space of tall buildings and led to the multi-tiered style of architecture exemplified by the Rockefeller Center (see **A-Z**).

Events:
January - New Year's Eve celebrations in Times Square (see **CITY SIGHTS**, **A-Z**); Boat Show. *February* - Dog Show; Chinese New Year. *March* - Cat Show; St Patrick's Day Parade. *Easter Sunday* - Easter Parade. *April* - Baseball season (see **Sport**). *May* - Ninth Avenue International Festival. *May-June* - Washington Square Outdoor Art Show. *June* - Museum Mile (all museums in upper Fifth Av free for three hours for one evening); Feast of St Anthony; Metropolitan Opera concerts in the park; Gay Pride Day Parade; Jazz Festival.
July - Summer pier concerts at South Street Seaport (see **CITY SIGHTS**, **A-Z**); Summer Garden at the Museum of Modern Art (see **ART GALLERIES**, **A-Z**); Shakespeare Festival in Central Park (see **Theatre**); *4 July* - Harbor Festival. *August* - Lincoln Center (see **MUSIC VENUES**, **A-Z**) Out of Doors

Festival; Harlem Week (see **Harlem**). *August-September* - Washington
Square Outdoor Art Show. *September* - US Open Tennis
Championships (see **Sport**); Feast of San Gennaro (see **Little Italy**);
New York is Book Country; Steuben Day Parade.
October - Columbus Day Parade; Halloween Day Parade; Knicks and
Rangers game (see **Sport**) at Madison Square Garden (see **A-Z**).
November - NYC Marathon; Thanksgiving Day Parade. *December* -
Christmas tree at the Rockefeller Center (see **A-Z**).
Check local press for details of the hundreds of ethnic and neighbour-
hood festivals held throughout the year (see **What's On**).

Excursions: One or two-day excursions to the following destinations
are recommended: Atlantic City, Saratoga, Lake George in upstate New
York, Fire Island/Montauk and Long Island (see **A-Z**). American Express
Travel Agency has nine branches in the city, including those at 65
Broadway (tel: 493-6500); 374 Park Av near 51st St. (tel: 421-8240);
Seaport Plaza, 100 Front St. (tel: 943-6947); and one in Bloomingdale's
(tel: 705-3171). See **Guides**, **Tours**.

Federal Hall National Memorial: This Parthenon-like building is
the spot where Washington took his oath of office as the first president
of the US. Now a museum and national monument, it has been a cus-
toms house and a bank. Open 0900-1630 Mon.-Fri. See WALK 4.

Ferries: The Circle Line Ferry will take you round Manhattan (see **A-
Z**) on a three and a half hour cruise from Pier 83 at the end of W 43rd
St. (see WALK 3). Circle Line Ferries also leave from Castle Clinton (see
A-Z) in Battery Park (see PARKS, WALK 4, **A-Z**) for Liberty Island and the
Statue of Liberty (see CITY SIGHTS, **A-Z**), tel: 269-5755 for info. Seaport
Line has a 90-min cruise around the tip of Manhattan leaving from Pier
16 at South St. The Staten Island Ferry (see CITY SIGHTS, **Staten Island**)
which leaves from Battery Park (see PARKS, **A-Z**) is good value at $0.25.

Flatiron Building: See SKYSCRAPERS.

Food: See RESTAURANTS, **Eating Out**.

Ford Foundation Building: This building at the east end of 42nd St. contains the first of NYC's indoor atriums, a semi-tropical garden set out between the L-shaped office blocks. See **WALK 3**.

Fraunces Tavern: Samuel Fraunces was an innkeeper who became steward to President Washington. He owned this tavern, at the corner of Pearl Street where Washington took leave of his officers at the end of the war. It is still a restaurant, serving great breakfasts, but also houses a Museum of the Revolutionary War and New York City. See **WALK 4**.

Frick Collection: The perfect museum to visit if you don't have much time to spare. The collection includes works by Van Dyck, Fragonard, Turner, Rembrandt, Whistler, El Greco and Gainsborough as well as Vermeer's *Officer and Laughing Girl*. It is also filled with 18thC furnishings and has a peaceful enclosed marble courtyard. There are free daily introductory talks and slide shows. See **ART GALLERIES**.

Gracie Mansion: This mansion, on East End Av at 88th St. in Carl Schurz Park (see **PARKS**), was built in 1799 by the Scottish merchant Alexander Gracie as his country house. It is now the residence of the Mayor of New York. Tours by appointment only.

Grand Central Station: The huge clock above the station entrance commemorates the railroad's founder Cornelius Vanderbilt (see **A-Z**). The Grand Concourse itself is immense and there is a night sky with star constellations painted on the ceiling. An acoustic phenomenon just outside the Oyster Bar (see **RESTAURANTS - MIDTOWN**) allows you to whisper in one corner and be heard at the other end of the wide space. Free tours of this fine Beaux Arts building on E 42nd St. (opposite Park Av), are organized by the Municipal Art Society and leave from the Kodak hoarding on Wednesdays at 1300. See **WALK 3**, **Railways**.

Grant's Tomb: The marble sepulchre of Ulysses S. Grant, Lincoln's successful supreme commander in the Civil War and President of the US between 1868-76, stands on Riverside Drive at W 122 St. in Harlem (see **CITY DISTRICTS**, **A-Z**).

Greenwich Village: This area was once a group of country estates. Before the First World War it was NYC's Bohemia and still has some of that atmosphere. See **CITY DISTRICTS, WALK 2**.

Guggenheim Museum: This amazing Frank Lloyd Wright building resembles an upside-down beehive - or a giant snail, or a corkscrew. The fourth floor houses a permanent collection of Cubist paintings. There are works by Chagall, Kandinsky, Klee and Léger. Paintings by Degas, Van Gogh and Cézanne, as well as Picasso's early *End of the Road* and *14th of July,* are contained in the Tannhauser Wing. See **ART GALLERIES**.

Guides: Brian Prinsell of Personal Transit offers tours, in a deluxe van, of all five boroughs (tel: 718-238-0133); Lou Singer of Singer's Tours specializes in tours of Brooklyn and Lower Manhattan, including Harlem (tel: 718-875-9084); and Vi Lefkoff of New York Knowhow organizes shopping and general interest tours (tel: 734-4132). See **Excursions**, **Tours**.

Guinness World Records Hall: This little museum, dedicated to the longest, shortest, highest, smallest, fattest, oldest, youngest and strangest achievements of mankind, was set up in the concourse of the Empire State Building (see **SKYSCRAPERS**, **A-Z**) when it was still the tallest building in the world.

Hairdressers: There are hairdressers of all kinds in all areas of the city. Ask at your hotel or check the Yellow Pages for nearby salons. The adventurous can try the Astor Place Barber Shop, at 2 Astor Pl at Eighth St. and Broadway, which offers New Wave haircuts and styles at reasonable prices (tel: 475-9354).

Hamilton Grange: The home of Alexander Hamilton, first US Secretary of the Treasury (featured on $10 bills), is situated in Hamilton Terrace on Convent Av at 142nd St., Harlem. Hamilton was killed in a duel by Aaron Burr who lived in the Morris-Jumel Mansion (see **A-Z**).

Harlem: This area, extending from 110th St. to the Harlem River, had its heyday in the jazz age of the 1920s and 30s when the Cotton Club was *the* place to be seen. There are several places worth visiting, including Audubon Terrace (see **A-Z**), home to several museums; the Cloisters (see **ART GALLERIES**, **A-Z**); the Harlem River Houses at 151st St.; Strivers' Row (on 138th St. between Eighth Av and Powell Boulevard), one of the finest terraces in New York; the Schomberg Center for Research in Black Culture at Lenox Av and 135th St.; the Abyssinian Baptist Church; Grant's Tomb (see **A-Z**); Hamilton Grange (see **A-Z**); and the Morris-Jumel Mansion (see **A-Z**). The Studio Museum at 2033 Fifth Av has a fine collection of Black art. For children, there is also Aunt Len's Doll and Toy Museum at 6 Hamilton Terrace at 141st St. (by appointment only). The Penny Sightseeing Company at 303 W 42nd St. organizes tours of Harlem (a good idea since it is not always safe to walk in some parts of the area). See **CITY DISTRICTS**.

Hayden Planetarium: Belongs to the Museum of Natural History (see **CHILDREN**, **A-Z**) and is mainly intended for the instruction and enjoyment of children. Laser shows on Friday nights. See **CHILDREN**.

Health: Standards of medical care in New York are high, but treatment is very expensive. It is therefore essential to take out adequate health insurance before leaving home (see **Insurance**).

Hospitals - Bellevue Hospital, First Av at 29th St. (tel: 561-4141); Manhattan Eye, Ear & Throat Hospital, 210 E 64th St. (tel: 838-9200); New York University Hospital, 550 First Av at 23rd St. (tel: 340-7300); Columbia Presbyterian Medical Center, Broadway at 168th St. (tel: 694-2500); Lenox Hill Hospital, Park Av at 77th St. (tel: 794-4567); St Vincent's, Seventh Av and W 11th St. (tel: 790-7000); Mount Sinai, Fifth Av at 100th St. (tel: 650-6500). See **Emergency Numbers**.

Helmsley Palace Hotel: Owned by the property developer Harry Helmsley, who also owns several other hotels which bear his name, the Helmsley Palace is famous for the clever incorporation of the beautiful 19thC Villard Houses whose splendidly lavish interiors now form the hotels public rooms. These mansions, based on the Cancelleria Palace in Venice, were originally built for the railroad owner Henry Villard.

Herald Square: This square, at the junction of Broadway with Sixth Av and 34th St., is the site of Macy's (see **SHOPPING 1**), the biggest department store in the world, as well as the Herald Center, a complex of boutiques and restaurants with observation elevators.

Hispanic Museum: Run by the Hispanic Society of America and located in Audubon Terrace (see **A-Z**). Besides an excellent collection of Spanish paintings, it houses artefacts and archeological remains from Iberia and South America. See **MUSEUMS 2**.

Hudson River: Flows along Manhattan's western side and divides New York City from Jersey City, and New York State from the State of New Jersey. The George Washington Bridge crosses the river from 178th St. in Manhattan to Fort Lee in New Jersey. Two toll tunnels run under the river: the Holland Tunnel, at Canal St. and Hudson St., and the Lincoln Tunnel on 42nd st. east of the Port Authority Terminal.

Insurance: You should take out adequate travel insurance covering you against theft and loss of property and money as well as medical expenses. Your travel agent should be able to recommend a suitable policy. See **Car Hire**, **Crime and Theft**, **Health**.

Intrepid Sea-Air-Space Museum: See WALK 3.

Johnson, Philip: The grand old man of US architecture who designed the Seagram Building (see SKYSCRAPERS, **A-Z**) along with Mies Van der Rohe; the New York State Theater (see **Lincoln Center**); the AT&T Building; the Citicorp Center (see SKYSCRAPERS, **A-Z**); and the extensions to the Museum of Modern Art (see ART GALLERIES, **A-Z**).

La Guardia, Henry F. : The NYC mayor who, from 1934 to 1946, cleaned up the city's administration after decades of corruption and scandal. One of New York's airports is named after him (see **Airports**).

Laundries: Self-service Laundromats charge $1.25 per load of washing and $1 per load of drying. Laundry rates in hotels are listed. Dry-cleaning costs $5 per suit and $2 per shirt.

Lincoln Center: The Lincoln Center for the Performing Arts, at 64th St. and Broadway between Columbus Av and Amsterdam Av, contains the Metropolitan Opera House; the Avery Fisher Hall, home of the NY Philharmonic Orchestra; the Alice Tully Hall, home of the Chamber Music Society; and the New York State Theater, home of the NYC Ballet and NYC Opera. It was opened in 1963 by John D. Rockefeller III (see **Rockefellers**), one of its main benefactors. See MUSIC VENUES.

'Little Church Around the Corner': Properly called the Church of the Transfiguration, the church earned its title in 1870 when the pastor of a church refused to perform a funeral service for an actor and suggested 'the little church around the corner' instead. See CHURCHES.

Little Italy: The main attractions of this district are its shops and restaurants. The main thoroughfare is Mulberry St., and the liveliest time of year to visit it is during the Feast of San Gennaro, a week of festivities in the month of September. See CITY DISTRICTS.

Long Island: The island is 125 miles long but only 23 miles across at its widest point. The villages along the north shore overlook harbours and beaches, and the cliffs are dotted with mansions built in the 1920s. Long, busy, sandy beaches stretch along the south shore. Long Island is the site of the quintessential suburban American development, Levittown. You can reach the island by train from Penn Station (see **Railways**) or by bus from the Port Authority Terminal (see **Buses**).

Lost Property: See **Taxis**.

McGraw-Hill Building: See **Rockefeller Centre**.

Madison Square: The original home of Madison Square Garden (see **A-Z**), and the former centre of New York City's theatre district, lies at the junction of Fifth Av and Broadway at 23rd St.
The New York Life Building now occupies the spot where the theatre stood, and the Flatiron Building (see **SKYSCRAPERS**) dominates the square's southern side.

Madison Square Garden: As its name suggests, Madison Square Garden was originally sited, in 1928, in Madison Square (see **A-Z**). This theatre, designed by Stanford White, has moved twice since and is now at 32nd St. above Penn Station (see **Railways**). In its heyday it was notorious as a place of scandal and debauchery. See **MUSIC VENUES**.

Manhattan: An island of some 22 square miles in area, surrounded by the Hudson (see **A-Z**), East (see **A-Z**) and Harlem rivers. It constitutes the central borough of New York, and contains most of the major attractions of the city. See **WALKS**.

Marble Collegiate Church: This Gothic church, with its marble exterior, belongs to the longest-established Protestant congregation in the USA, which was founded in 1628 by the Dutch West India Company. Peter Minuit, Governor of Nieuw Amsterdam, was the first church elder and Norman Vincent Peale, famous author of *The Power of Positive Thinking*, was pastor here for over 50 years. See **CHURCHES**.

Markets:

Food - stalls between 111th St. and 116th St. on Park Av in Spanish Harlem specialize in Mediterranean foods; a covered market in Essex St. in the Lower East Side offers a wide range of different kinds of food-stuff; there are also greenmarkets, run by the city, which sell local farm produce at various locations around town, such as the World Trade Center (see **SKYSCRAPERS**, **A-Z**) and Union Square.

Clothes - on Sundays stalls selling clothes appear in Orchard St. in the Lower East Side; the SoHo Emporium at 375 W Broadway contains dozens of stalls selling unusual handcrafted clothing and jewellery at reasonable prices; Unique Warehouse at 718 Broadway and Astor Pl specializes in vintage clothes, T-shirt painting and the latest trends for the young.

Collectables - the Annex Antiques Fair & Flea Market at 26th St. and Sixth Av offers nostalgia items, antiques and curiosities (Sun.); the out-door Canal Street Flea Market at 335 Canal St. is good for antiques and jewellery (weekends from Mar.-Nov.); another flea market on Columbus Av, between 76th St. and 77th St., deals in everything - books, records, film posters, jewellery, clothes. See **Best Buys**, **Shopping**.

Metropolitan Museum of Art: This huge museum houses five main collections, namely European Paintings, American Paintings, Medieval Art, Primitive Art and the Egyptian Collection. Highlights of these are the Temple of Dendur in the Egyptian Wing on the first floor, and Tiffany stained-glass windows and Sargent's *Madame X* in the American Wing (on three floors). The outstanding European galleries on the second floor include the André Meyer Galleries containing 19thC works with emphasis on the Impressionists and Post-Impressionists (eg Van Gogh's *Sunflowers* and *Cypresses*, Rodin's *Hand of God*, Degas' *14-Year-Old Little Dancer*). The new Tisch Galleries, housed in a five-storey wing containing European sculpture and decorative art, host major exhibitions. The museum has gift shops, a restaurant and a café. There are free conducted tours and tape tours of the main attractions as well as of specific areas. See **ART GALLERIES, WALK 1.**

Midtown: This huge area between 14th St. and 59th St. takes in New

York's Theater District (see **CITY DISTRICTS**), including Broadway (see **A-Z**); the prestigious shops along Fifth Av; most of the city's hotels; great landmarks, such as the Chrysler Building (see **SKYSCRAPERS**, **WALK 3**, **A-Z**) and the Citicorp Center (see **SKYSCRAPERS**, **A-Z**); many major museums; the Port Authority Bus Terminal (see **WALK 3**, **Buses**), and Penn and Grand Central Stations (see **Railways**, **A-Z**). See **Orientation**.

Money: You can change currency and traveller's cheques at banks and bureaux de change, although many banks will only cash cheques for their own customers. Check beforehand if they charge a fee or commission (some don't!) and what these are likely to be. Bank Leumi Trust Company of New York, 579 Seventh Av and Deak New York Inc., 630 Fifth Av both specialize in exchange services, and many of the offices of international banks, such as Citibank and Chemical Bank, will change currency at standard rates. All the major credit cards (American Express, Mastercharge/Access, Visa, Diners Club and Carte Blanche) are readily accepted in hotels, restaurants, shops and by car-hire firms. If you should lose a credit card call the relevant office immediately (American Express card holders should tel: 1-800-528-2121). See **Currency**, **Opening Times**, **Traveller's Cheques**.

Morris-Jumel Mansion: This mansion, on Edgecombe Av at W 160th St. in Harlem, was built as the country house of Roger Morris in 1765 and is decorated and furnished in the style of the period. Aaron

Burr, the tempestuous Federal-period politician who killed Alexander Hamilton in a dual, lived here during his retirement from politics. There are tours of the house, and its gardens are pleasant for picnics.

Museum of Modern Art (MOMA): Established in 1929, this permanent collection of painting, sculpture, design, drawing, photography, and film tracing the development of modern art from 1880, has undergone recent renovation and expansion. Enjoy the outdoor Sculpture Garden at ground level which contains statues by Henry Moore, Matisse and Rodin as well as Picasso's *She Goat*. Among the outstanding Impressionist and Post-Impressionist works on the first floor are Van Gogh's *Starry Night* and Rousseau's *Sleeping Gypsy*. There are separate rooms for Monet's *Water Lilies*, Cubist paintings (some by Picasso and Braque) and works by Matisse. More modern American and abstract paintings and sculptures occupy the second floor, including works by Frank Stella, Andrew Wyeth, Hopper, Andy Warhol and the New York School artists, Pollock, De Kooning, and Rothko. On the third floor, the emphasis is on architecture and design with models of modern building, examples of Tiffany glasswork and Art Nouveau furniture. There are also galleries devoted to one of the most interesting collections of photographs in the world. Two theatres regularly show films, and there is a gift shop and a Garden Café (overlooking the Sculpture Garden). See ART GALLERIES.

Museums: New York City has museums to suit every taste and interest. In addition to those listed in MUSEUMS and described here in the A-Z, the following are recommended: the Numismatic Society in Audubon Terrace (see A-Z), Japan House, 333 E 47th St., and the Library and Museum of the Performing Arts in the Lincoln Center (see A-Z), 111 Amsterdam Av.

Newspapers: Daily newspapers include the *New York Times*, an American institution, and a traditional armful of reading, which offers the best international coverage; the *New York Post*, containing local news and scandal; the *Daily News*, New York's 'hometown paper' with good local news coverage and gossip; *New York Newsday*, mostly appealing to Queens and Long Island (see **A-Z**) suburbanites; and the business-orientated *Wall Street Journal*. See **What's On**.

New York Conventions and Visitors Bureau: See WALK 3, Tourist Information.

New York Historical Society: 19thC American paintings (especially the landscapes of the Hudson River School artists), watercolours by the ornithologist James Audubon and lamps by Louis Tiffany are just some of the attractions in this collection housed on five floors. The museum also contains a reference library of works on American history, maps and prints tracing the development of the city from colonial times, and displays of horsedrawn carriages. See MUSEUMS 2.

New York Public Library: You cannot miss this building, on Fifth Av between 41st St. and 42nd St., fronted as it is by two large stone lions representing *Patience* and *Fortitude*. The library runs an excellent reference service, and you can see some of the most splendid public rooms in the city on one of the popular conducted tours (1100-1400 Mon.-Sat.). See WALK 3.

New York Stock Exchange: The home of the 'junk bond' and the 'big bang' stands on the corner of Wall St. and Broad St. You can view the Great Hall, the floor where the financial dealings are carried out, from a visitors' gallery, while the Visitors' Center provides up-to-date information on the workings of the exchange. See WALK 4.

Olmsted, Frederick Law: The architect who, along with his partner Calvert Vaux, won the competition to design Central Park (see CITY SIGHTS, PARKS, WALK 1, A-Z). He planned it as a rural paradise, with the Utopian dream of bringing the countryside into the lives of the people of Manhattan (see A-Z). Vaux and Olmsted also designed Riverside Park (see PARKS), Morningside Park and Prospect Park (see PARKS, A-Z).

Olympic Tower: The black glass exterior of this block on Fifth Av reflects St Patrick's Cathedral which stands nearby (see CHURCHES, A-Z).

It contains one of the many public atriums in New York City.

Opening Times:

Bars - 0800/0900 (noon at latest) till 0400 Mon.-Sat., till 0300 Sun. although some shut earlier (see **BARS**). *Shops* - 1000-1800 Mon.-Sat. (till 2100 Thurs.), 1200-1800 Sun. (see **SHOPPING**, **Shopping**). *Banks* - 0900-1500 Mon.-Fri. Some also Sat. am (see **Money**). There are also 24-hr automatic teller machines. *Post offices* - 0800-1600 (see **A-Z**).

Orientation:

New York is an easy city in which to find your way around. This is especially true of the area of Manhattan (see **A-Z**) north of 14th St., which is laid out on a grid system composed of avenues, which run north and south, and streets, which run east and west. Fifth Av divides the east side from the west side of town. Uptown (see **A-Z**) is north of 59th St., downtown (see **A-Z**) is to the south of 14th St and midtown (see **A-Z**) is in between. The numbering of buildings east or west starts at Fifth Av (eg 1 E Eighth St. is just east of Fifth Av, and 1 W Eighth St. is just west of Fifth Av).

Equip yourself with a detailed street map as well as bus and subway maps. If you are walking anywhere it will take at least 15 min to cover ten blocks going north or south. Those running east and west take longer. See **Buses**, **Ferries**, **Subway**, **Taxis**, **Transport**.

Paddy's Market: See WALK 3.

Paley Park: This much-loved little park has a waterfall which delightfully dulls the sound of the traffic. It is named after William Paley, chairman of CBS, who founded the Museum of Broadcasting (see CHILDREN) next door. See PARKS.

Pan Am Building: This striking building was designed by Mies Van der Rohe who modelled the tall black structure on the shape of an aeroplane wing. It towers over Grand Central Station (see WALK 3, Railways, A-Z) and shuts off Park Av to the south.

Parking: Read signs carefully before parking since it is expensive to reclaim a car that has been towed away. There are municipal car parks (parking lots) on Eighth Av at 53rd St.; Manhattan Civic Center; Sixth Av; Park Row; Broome St. between Ludlow St. and Essex St.; Leonard St. between Lafayette St. and Centre St.; Essex St. north of Delancey St. They cost approximately $2 per hr. Kinney is the best-known chain of private car parks - over 10,000 parking places in 100 convenient locations in the metropolitan area. Prices are displayed in front (approximately $6 per hr, $20 per day).

Passports: Valid passports and visas are required by overseas visitors.

Pets: Household pets are allowed into the USA when they have been inoculated against rabies between a month and a year prior to entry, and are accompanied by the appropriate documentation.
24-hr emergency medical treatment for pets - Animal Medical Center, 510 E 62nd St. between York Av and FDR Dr (tel: 838-800).

Pierpoint Morgan Library: The prominent banker J. P. Morgan had this building built to hold his massive collection of medieval manuscripts, Renaissance books and works of art. His son J. P. Jnr gifted the library and building to the public in 1924. The best pieces from the collection are displayed in the original library. See MUSEUMS 1.

Plaza Hotel: The hotel is named after Grand Army Plaza at the south-west corner of Central Park (see **CITY SIGHTS**, **PARKS**, **WALK 1**, **A-Z**) and one of NYC's most popular hotels. The famous Oak Bar offers refuge from the bustle of Fifth Av.

Police: See **Crime and Theft**, **Emergency Numbers**.

Port Authority Terminal: See **Buses**.

Post Offices: The main post office at 34th St. and Eighth Av is open 24 hours a day, seven days a week (tel: 967-8585). The other major midtown post office is at 45th St. and Lexington Av. It costs $0.90 per oz ($0.45 per 1/2 oz) to post a letter overseas and $0.25 for destinations within the US and Canada. See **Opening Times**, **Telephones and Telegrams**.

Public Holidays: New Year's Day (1 Jan.), Martin Luther King Day (third Mon. in Jan.), Presidents' Day (third Mon. in Feb.), Memorial Day (last Mon. in May), Independence Day (4 July), Labor Day (first

Mon. in Sept.), Columbus Day (second Mon. in Oct.), Thanksgiving Day (last Thurs. in Nov.), Christmas Day (25 Dec.).
Most shops are closed on New Year's Day, Thanksgiving Day and Christmas Day. On other holidays shops stay open for special sales and bars are open until 0400. See **Events**.

Queens: This is the largest borough in New York City. The Astoria area is a good place to sample Greek cuisine while Jackson Heights is the spot to find South American food. Jamaica Bay is a bird-watchers' paradise (some 300 varieties of fowl to be seen), and the Rockaways, which encloses the bay, is a ten-mile stretch of beaches.

Radio City Music Hall: See **Rockefeller Center**.

Railways: Trains services to upstate New York, Boston and New England depart from Grand Central Station (see **WALK 3**, **A-Z**) on 42nd St. at Park Av, tel: 532-4900. The station's meeting point and round information booth are both situated in the main hall beside the clock. There are underground connections from here to other buildings. Amtrak trains to Washington DC, the Long Island Railroad and the New Jersey Transit all leave from Penn Station at 33rd St. and Seventh Av (tel: 868-8970). Trains are generally clean and punctual. See **Smoking**.

Religious Services: Every possible religious affiliation is represented in New York. Call the following numbers for information:

Roman Catholic	371-1000.
Episcopalian	316-7400.
Islamic	533-5060.
Jewish	753-2288.
Lutheran	532-6350.
Presbyterian	870-2000.

Consult the Manhattan Yellow Pages for the addresses and telephone numbers of many more churches and temples.

Riverside Church: Climb the 400-ft tower of this Gothic revival church, inspired by the French cathedral of Chartres and financed by

John D. Rockefeller Jnr (see **Rockefellers**), for one of the most impressive views of the city skyline. Carillon (the largest set in the world) recitals on Saturdays and holidays. See **CHURCHES**.

Rockefeller Center: The main building at the heart of this complex, stretching from 48th St. to 52nd St. and Fifth Av to Seventh Av, is the RCA Building, home of the NBC studios and the famous Rainbow Room Restaurant. The plaza in front of the RCA Building is an ice-skating rink in winter and an outdoor restaurant in summer (note the huge statue of *Prometheus* with his torch). At Christmas time a large tree is erected in front of the RCA Building, the Channel Gardens are extravagantly decorated with angels and the restaurants and stores throng with Christmas shoppers (see **Events**).

One of the complex's finest structures is the Radio City Music Hall, a National Landmark building with a splendid Art Deco interior - so splendid, in fact, that murals from the men's toilets are now in the Museum of Modern Art (see **ART GALLERIES**, **A-Z**). There are interesting backstage tours of this 'showplace of the nation', the world's largest indoor theatre (tel: 757-3100).

The McGraw-Hill Building on the other side of Fifth Av between 48th St. and 49th St. houses The New York Experience, a multi-media celebration of the history of NY. See **CITY SIGHTS**, **Rockefellers**.

Rockefellers: One of New York's, and America's, wealthiest and most powerful families. The family fortune was first amassed by John D. Rockefeller who established Standard Oil (Esso) as the leading oil company. His son, John D. Rockefeller Jnr, put his father's multi-millions to good use, assisting in the financing of the Riverside Church (see CHURCHES, **A-Z**) and agreeing to build a new opera house for the Metropolitan Opera. The latter ended up, with the help of John D. Rockefeller III, in the Lincoln Center (see MUSIC VENUES, **A-Z**). Nelson A. Rockefeller was governor of New York State from 1958-74, and vice-president from 1974-76.

Roosevelt Island: Formerly known as Blackwell Island, after the family who farmed the island and lived in the clapboard farmhouse on Main St. from 1796 to 1804 (open to the public). It became known as Welfare Island when the city administration established a prison, hospitals, a poorhouse and a lunatic asylum here. Now it is a pleasant residential area. You can reach it by tram from 60th St. and Second Av.

St Bartholomew's Church: This large ornate church stands at Park Av and 51st St. The Sunday afternoon concerts held here in autumn and winter are justly famous. There are also concerts at noon on Wednesdays.

St John the Divine: Construction began in 1892 on this huge Gothic cathedral, but one third of the building is still unfinished. You can watch the masons at work cutting and carving stones using medieval methods, visit the Biblical Garden, or attend one of the regular concerts held here. See CHURCHES.

St Mark's-in-the-Bowery: This church was built, in 1799, on the site of Peter Stuyvesant's chapel, on his farm or *bouwerie,* and he is buried under the cobbled yard. The church was damaged by fire in 1979 and is undergoing restoration. See CHURCHES.

St Patrick's Cathedral: This famous Gothic cathedral was designed by James Renwick and seats 2500 people. The white marble

and stone exterior is over 300 ft high and is studded with intense blue stained-glass windows. Walk round to the back to visit the Lady Chapel and the crypt, which houses the remains of former cardinals. Look out for the ceremonial red cardinals' caps suspended from the ceiling in the sanctuary. See **CHURCHES**.

St Paul's Chapel: The oldest church (1766) in Manhattan (see **A-Z**) resembles St Martin-in-the-Fields in Trafalgar Square in London. This was George Washington's place of worship and his pew can be seen in the north aisle. Original Waterford crystal chandeliers light the interior. Classical music concerts are held here. See **CHURCHES**, **WALK 4**.

St Peter's: See **CHURCHES**, **Citicorp Center**.

St Thomas's Church: This slightly lopsided Gothic church, on Fifth Av at W 53rd St., has interesting carvings over its doors - there is, for example, a $ entwined in the lovers' knot above the Bride's Door! You can hear choral music here at noon on Wednesdays and organ recitals on Sunday afternoons.

Seagram Building: This deceptively simple building, the first in the

Modernist style, has been widely copied. Its architects, Philip Johnson and Mies Van der Rohe, paid close attention to detail. A huge theatre backcloth by Picasso decorates the famous Four Seasons Restaurant. There are guided tours on Tuesdays at 1500. See **SKYSCRAPERS**.

Shopping: New York City is a showcase for the world's merchandise. You'll find branches of all the famous retail chains here as well as every kind of specialty shop imaginable. The best shopping and browsing areas are in SoHo (see **CITY DISTRICTS**, **A-Z**) and the Lower East Side (Manhattan's bargain basement), on Fifth Av (34th St. to 59th St.), Madison Av (59th St. to 72nd St.) and Columbus Av (72nd St. to 86th St.). There are antique shops in the east 50s and 80s along Madison Av in SoHo, but the ones in Brooklyn along Atlantic Av, between Hoyt St. and Third St., are generally cheaper. A city sales tax of 8.25% is levied on every purchase. See **SHOPPING**, **Best Buys**, **Markets**, **Opening Times**.

Smoking: New NYC laws prohibit smoking in public places such as theatres, lobbies, office buildings, etc. There is no smoking on elevators, in subways or on trains or buses. Restaurants must provide both smoking and non-smoking areas.

SoHo: The name of this area is short for **So**uth of **Ho**uston (pronounced 'Howstin') and is synonymous in NYC with art galleries. It was once inhabited by the trendy crowd who moved here from Greenwich Village. They were displaced by the monied set who gradually followed them here, driving them on to the district of TriBeCa (see **A-Z**). In contrast, the enduring thing about SoHo is its cast-iron buildings - those in Greene Street are excellent examples, but you should also look out for the Haughwout Building at Broome and Broadway, and the Little Singer Building on Prince and Broadway. See **CITY DISTRICTS**.

South Street Seaport: The centre of this area, on the eastern tip of Manhattan (see **A-Z**), is occupied by Piers 15-18 where several sailing ships are moored. You can also take a three-hour cruise round the harbour in summer on the schooner *Pioneer*. One of the district's liveliest spots is the Fulton Fish Market which must be visited extremely early in the morning (0500). A good introduction to the district is provided by The Seaport Experience which regularly screens a film tracing the area's history from the 19thC. Schermerhorn Row contains some of the oldest buildings in New York, including warehouses and two seafood restaurants, called Sweet's and Sloppy Louie's, which recreate the service, but not the prices, provided to traders and sailors in the past. There are also a large number of interesting shops selling items relating to the trades and crafts of the Seaport's heyday. See **CITY SIGHTS**, **WALK 4**.

Sport: *Spectator sports*: Baseball - Shea Stadium in Queens, home of the New York Mets; Yankee Stadium in the Bronx, home of the New York Yankees.
Basketball - Madison Square Garden (Nov.-Apr.). Tel: 563-80-00 for tickets for a New York Knicks game.
Football - Meadowlands Stadium, East Rutherford, NJ. Tel: 421-66-00 for tickets for the New York Jets games and 201-935-8222 for tickets to see the Giants play.
Ice hockey - Madison Square Garden (Oct.-Apr.). Tel: 563-80-00 for tickets for a New York Rangers game.
Tennis - Flushing Meadow Park, Queens. Venue of the US Open Tennis Championships (end of Aug.). Tel: 718-592-8000 for tickets (subway 7 to Shea Stadium/Willets Point).
Horse racing - Aqueduct Racetrack in Ozone Park, Queens (Oct.-May); Belmont, in Elmont on Long Island (May-Aug., Sept.-Oct.). Harness racing (trotting) takes place in Yonkers; Roosevelt Raceway in Westbury, Long Island; Meadowlands, East Rutherford, New Jersey. Check times with the New York Racing Association (tel: 718-641-4700).
Participatory sports: Golf - Island's End Golf Course, North Road, Greenport NY 11944.
Fishing - Hudson River off Manhattan along the Riverside Park esplanade from W 72nd to 84th St. and from W 91st St. to 100th St. Charter fishing boats from Betty W, 3030 Emmons Av.
Swimming - Outdoor public pools at 59th St. and West End Av, and at the East River at 77th St. Also check with the local YMCAs.
Tennis - There are more than 500 public tennis courts in the Big Apple. Tel: 360-8133 for information on those in Manhattan.

Horse riding - Claremont Riding Academy, 175 W 89th St., Central Park (tel: 724-5100); Van Cortlandt Riding Stables, Broadway at 254th St., the Bronx (tel: 543-4433); Cullmitt Stables, 51 Caton Place at E Eighth St., Prospect Park, Brooklyn (tel: 718-438-8849).

Staten Island: This once-rural borough became suburbanized with the opening of the Verrazano Narrows Bridge (see **A-Z**) in 1964. However, you can still visit Staten Island the old-fashioned way on the ferry (see CITY SIGHTS, **Ferries**). Bus M113 will take you from the dingy terminal to the two most interesting sites on the island: The Jacques Marchais Center for Tibetan Art, 338 Lighthouse Av, Richmond, and the Richmondtown Restoration, 441 Clarke Av, Richmondtown. The former houses a remarkably complete collection of bronzes, paintings and musical instruments inside Buddhist temple buildings. The latter is an 18thC working village where you can watch the skills and techniques of the period being demonstrated. There is also a Children's Museum, and a Zoo which has a notable collection of rare rattlesnakes.

Statue of Liberty: 3.5 million visitors each year head out to *Liberty Enlightening the World* (the full name of Frederic Auguste Bartholdi's statue) on the Circle Line Ferry (see **Ferries**) so expect long queues (you

should allow about four hours for the visit). The enormous statue of Lady Liberty, the interior iron framework of which was engineered by Alexandre Gustave Eiffel, was restored for her 100th birthday in 1986. A museum containing displays on the restoration, as well as on immigration, is located in the base which is emblazoned with Emma Lazarus' poem *New Colossus*, the most famous lines of which are: 'Give me your tired, your poor/ Your huddled masses yearning to breathe free'. Call 363-3200 for information. See **CITY SIGHTS**.

Subway: The subway operates 24 hours a day, seven days a week, and each day 3.5 million passengers travel on it. The fare is a flat $1 and there are no concession passes or weekly tickets. You can purchase subway tokens at the booths in the stations (stock up on them since they can be used on buses too - see **Buses**). The subway provides the fastest means of travelling long distance across town, but stations offer few amenities apart from some telephones, benches and a few stores in the bigger ones. Both the stations and the system are undergoing refurbishment with the addition of new subway cars and the cleaning up of graffiti under Mayor Koch's special programmes. Although the subway is relatively safe during rush hours avoid travelling alone on it at night. Trains are designated either by letter or number (depending on which company they originally belonged to). A good map of the subway system is an essential item. See **Crime and Theft**, **Smoking**, **Transport**.

Taxes: See **Accommodation**, **Shopping**.

Taxis: Although there are 11,787 taxis in New York City, it is hard to find a cab during rush hours and in rainy weather. Make sure the cab you hail is a licensed and metered yellow cab (identifiable by the medallion on top). The light on the roof indicates when the cab is for hire. The fare starts at $1.15 and accumulates at the rate of $0.15 per ninth of a mile and every 14 seconds waiting in traffic. There is a $0.50 surcharge between 2000-0800 and you will be expected to give a tip (see **Tipping**). The average taxi fare for a journey across town works out at around $4 (up to four people can share a cab for the same fare), midtown to uptown is approximately $6, and midtown to downtown is about $10 (drivers do not like changing $10 or $20 bills). Take the computerized printout receipt you are given when you leave the taxi as it has the number of the cab and phone numbers for lost articles or complaints (tel: 382-9031 if you have a complaint, tel: 869-4513 if you lose something).

Telephones and Telegrams: There are plenty of public telephones on street corners and in restaurants, hotels, bars, etc. These take coins. Local calls cost $0.25 for the first three minutes and $0.10 for each block of three minutes thereafter. The area code for Manhattan and the Bronx is 212. Telephones have letters alongside the numbers on the dial or keys and some services use words instead of numbers (eg 01-800 CASH NOW is the American Express traveller's cheque information number).

Reverse charge call (collect call)   0 + 1 + area code + number.
Directory enquires   (Manhattan)   411 (free).
                      (other boroughs)   1-718-555-1212.
International dialling instructions   1-800-874-4000 (free).
Hotels usually levy additional charges on phone calls. Check what these are before making any calls (especially overseas).

Telegrams (cables) can be sent by phone through Western Union on 800-325-4045 or 344-8910, or from post offices (see **A-Z**). There is also a public fax machine in the lobby of the Empire State Building (see **SKYSCRAPERS**, **A-Z**).

Temple Emanu-El: America's largest synagogue and New York City's leading Reform synagogue is on Fifth Av at 65th St. You can visit it daily 1000-1700.

Theater Museum: This museum, in the arcade of the Minskoff Theater at 1515 Broadway, contains a collection of memorabilia originally housed in the Museum of the City of New York (1200-2000 Wed.-Sat.,1300-1700 Sun.).

Theatre: Although it can be expensive (see **Budget**) you should not leave without going to a few performances. Call NYC/ONSTAGE, 587-1111 (see **Telephones and Telegrams**) for recorded theatre information for both on and off-Broadway. Theatre tickets may be purchased directly from the box office or by writing in advance. Call Telecharge 239-6200 or Teletron 246-0102 to charge tickets by phone (there is a surcharge for this service). Ticket Central at W 42nd St. sells tickets for off-Broadway shows and the TKTS booth at the north end of Times Square (see **CITY SIGHTS**, **WALK 3**, **A-Z**) sells discounted theatre tickets for performances both on and off-Broadway. (If you don't mind queueing and are willing to take a chance you can get half-price tickets after 1500 for evening performances, and after 1000 for matinees on Wed., Sat. and Sun.) There is another TKTS booth at No. 2 World Trade Center (1100-1730 Mon.-Fri., 1100-1530 Sat.). The kiosk in Bryant Park (see **PARKS**, **A-Z**) specializes in music and dance tickets. A large selection of free 'twofer' coupons are available at the NY Visitors Bureau (see **Tourist Information**), which give about a third discount off tickets for a selection of longer-running shows when you purchase them at the theatre box office. 'Shakespeare in the Park' at the Delacorte Theater in Central Park (see **WALK 1**) makes a wonderful evening's entertainment in the summer (Tues.-Sun., June -Sept.). Queue by the theatre for the free tickets that are distributed at 1800 - be there by 1400 to collect a coupon -

for performances at 2000. See **Culture**, **What's On**.

Time Difference: Five hours ahead of GMT.

Times Square: Originally called Longacre Square, the area was renamed after the old building at No. 1 Times Square, which is the former home of the *New York Times*. Although the square is slightly seedy, it has a magical quality at night, with all the billboards, theatre queues and neon lights. Besides being at the centre of New York's Theater District (see CITY DISTRICTS), it is also the place New Yorkers come to celebrate New Year (see **Events**). See CITY SIGHTS, WALK 3, **Broadway**.

Tipping: In restaurants you should leave between 15-20% of the total bill as a tip. Taxi drivers expect at least a 20% tip and porters and bell-hops should be given around $1 per item of luggage.

Toilets: These can be found in public buildings such as museums, stations, shopping centres, etc. Those in bars and restaurants can also be used, although some have a 'patrons only' sign.

Tourist Information: You can get up-to-date information on events, programmes, shops and restaurants throughout the city as well

as obtain free bus, subway and tour maps, 'twofer' coupons (see **Theatre**) and sightseeing brochures at the New York Convention and Visitors Bureau. Although they can also advise on accommodation they do not make hotel bookings. The offices are at 2 Columbus Circle (tel: 212-397-8222) and 2 Times Sq at 42nd St. between Broadway and Seventh Av (0900-1800 Mon.-Fri., 1000-1800 Sat., Sun. and hol.).

Tours: *Bus tours* - Gray Line, 900 Eighth Av at 54th St., tel: 397-2600; Shortline,166 W 46th St., tel: 354-5122. Call 718-330-1234 for information on cultural tours and shoppers' buses.
Scheduled helicopter flights - Island Helicopters on E 34th St., tel: 683-4575; Manhattan Helicopters on W 30th St., tel: 247-8687. Expensive, but very enjoyable.
Walking tours - Walk of the Town, tel: 772-5927; Museum of the City of New York (see **CHILDREN, MUSEUMS 1**), tel: 534-1672; Harlem Spirituals, tel: 302-2594; Municipal Arts Society, tel: 935-3960; NY Historical Society (see **MUSEUMS 2, A-Z**), tel: 873-0125; Urban Park Rangers conduct free tours of Central Park (see **CITY SIGHTS, PARKS, WALK 1, A-Z**) every weekend, tel: 360-1333; Shorewalkers, 92nd St. YMCA, tel: 966-1100; Talk-A-Walk cassette tapes, tel: 686-0356. See **Excursions, Guides**.

Transport: Walking is the best means of seeing New York City. The subway (see **A-Z**) is fast and therefore best for longer distances, but not always very pleasant. Taxis (see **A-Z**) are plentiful and can be an adventure. See **Buses, Ferries, Orientation, Railways**.

Traveller's Cheques: American Express and Visa traveller's cheques in US dollars are accepted by banks, hotels, most shops and restaurants. Identification required. See **Crime and Theft, Currency, Money**.

TriBeCa: The name of this area is short for **Tri**angle **Be**low **Ca**nal (St.). Artists and warehouse converters moved here from SoHo (see **CITY DISTRICTS, A-Z**) and now the better-off are following them. As in SoHo, the cast-iron buildings (see **A-Z**) are an attractive feature of the area. See **CITY DISTRICTS**.

Trinity Church: This Episcopal church on Broadway at Wall St. is dwarfed by the twin towers of the World Trade Center (see **SKYSCRAPERS**, **A-Z**). It houses the graves of Robert Fulton, the inventor of the steamboat, and Alexander Hamilton, first Secretary of the Treasury. Concerts are held on Tuesdays. See **CHURCHES**, **WALK 4**.

Trump Tower: This huge block containing 230 apartments, all of which have views on three sides, is named after the developer Donald Trump who lives here (along with many other multi-millionaires). The Bonwit Teller department store (see **SHOPPING 1**) is situated in the building's atrium of shops and restaurants. See **SKYSCRAPERS**.

Tudor City: Composed of a group of 12 (supposedly Tudor-style) buildings ranging from ten to 32 storeys in height, which surrounds a little park at the east end of 42nd St. behind the United Nations (see **CITY SIGHTS**, **WALK 3**, **A-Z**). Their turrets are best seen from the East River (see **A-Z**) as you cruise past on a Circle Line Ferry (see **Ferries**).

TV and Radio: *TV* channels - Channel 2 CBS, Channel 4 NBC, Channel 5 WNYW, Channel 7 ABC, Channel 9 WWOR, Channel 11 WPIX and Channel 13 WPBS. Check the daily newspapers for complete television listings including cable TV, HBO (Home Box Office), Cinemax, ESPN (all sports) and CNN (all news). Free tickets to TV shows are available by writing or calling the networks concerned. *AM* Radio stations - news on WINS (1010) and CBS (880); talk shows on WOR (710) and WABC (770); sport on WFAN (660 AM). *FM* Radio Stations - classical music on WNCN (104.5), WQXR (103.5) and WNYC (93.9); rock music on WNEW (102.7), WXRK (92.3 KROCK) and WWPR (95.5); light music on WLTW (106.7) and WNSR (105.1); jazz on WKCR (89.9) and WBGO (88.3); and 'urban contemporary' on WRKS (98.7 KISSFM), WBLS (107.5) and WQHT (103.5).

United Nations: The Secretariat Building is the most easily identifiable as it is the tallest of the United Nations Headquarters complex. The low-lying domed building is the General Assembly where mem-

bers of the public can attend General Assembly meetings. Other attractions include the gardens, Chagall's stained-glass windows, and the delegates' dining room. See **CITY SIGHTS, WALK 3**.

Uptown: Anywhere north of 59th St. is uptown. In directions, it can refer to anywhere north of where you are at present. See **Orientation**.

Vanderbilts: Along with the Astors (see **A-Z**) and the Rockefellers (see **A-Z**), the Vanderbilts are one of the three most famous families in New York. Their fortune was amassed by the infamous 'Commodore' Cornelius (his rank came from running the Staten Island Ferry - see **CITY SIGHTS**) who ruthlessly exploited the development of steamships and railroads. His son William inherited $100 million from him in 1877, and doubled that sum within eight years. Gertrude Whitney, the Commodore's granddaughter, was an excellent sculptor and a patron of the arts. Her collection forms the basis of the Whitney Museum (see **ART GALLERIES, A-Z**). Gloria Vanderbilt is a well known fashion designer.

Verrazano Narrows Bridge: One of the longest single-span bridges in the world links Brooklyn (see **A-Z**) to Staten Island (see **A-Z**) over the stretch of water named after the explorer Giovanni di Verrazano who first sighted the estuary of the Hudson River in 1524.

Villard Houses: See **Helmsley Palace Hotel**.

Waldorf-Astoria: This is possibly the best-known hotel in New York. This site, at 301 Park Av between 49th St. and 50th St., is the hotel's second home. Originally two hotels, the Waldorf and the Astoria, stood at 34th St., where the Empire State Building (see **SKYSCRAPERS, A-Z**) is now.

Washington Square: The area now occupied by Washington Square, at the heart of Greenwich Village (see **CITY DISTRICTS, WALK 2, A-Z**), was once a duck marsh, then a paupers' cemetery and finally a parade ground before town houses were built on it in 1836 and solid members of society took up residence here. The architectural style of that period is preserved only on the north side of the square which is now the centre of New York University. Stanford White's Triumphal Arch, originally made of wood, was erected in 1889 to commemorate the centenary of Washington's inauguration. It was replaced by a stone arch in 1892. Statues of Washington, both in and out of uniform, adorn the north side of the arch. Garibaldi, another great soldier and politician, is also memorialized in stone. See **WALK 2**.

What's On: The weekly *New York Magazine* lists restaurants, museums, theatre and cinema programmes, music and dance venues, sales and bargains (and 'Best Bets'). *City Guide Magazine* is a free weekly journal of highlights, sightseeing attractions, Broadway shows, etc which is distributed to hotels. The weekly (every Wed.) 'Cheap Thrills' section of the *Village Voice* is a guide to NYC events which often lists more unusual happenings. Check the *New York Times* for first-run films (Fri. and Sun.). The *Daily News* Sunday 'City Lights' section provides guides to the arts and entertainment. See **Newspapers**.

Whitney Museum of American Art: This museum, designed by Marcel Breuer and founded by Gertrude Vanderbilt Whitney (see **Vanderbilts**), houses wonderfully provocative exhibitions of 20thC American art - such as Calder's mobiles and stabiles. The permanent collection includes the Abstract Expressionists: high priests Pollock and De Kooning, Ad Reinhard's *Black Painting*, Warhol's *Coke Bottles* and Jasper John's *Three Flags*. There is another branch, with changing exhibits, at the Equitable Center, 51st St. and Seventh Av, where Roy Lichtenstein's *Mural With Blue Brushstroke* and Thomas Hart Benton's *America Today* adorn the huge lobby (1100-1800 Mon.-Fri., till 1930 Thurs., 1200-1600 Sat.; free). A third branch at Philip Morris, 42nd St. and Park Av, features a Sculpture Court, changing exhibits and a café (see **WALK 3**). There is a fourth branch for temporary exhibitions at 33 Maiden Lane, Federal Reserve Plaza. See **ART GALLERIES**.

Woolworth Building: This building, facing City Hall Park across Broadway (see **A-Z**), is one of the most popular buildings in New York. Designed for Frank W. Woolworth (of the famous chain of shops), it celebrates his commercial success in a Gothic style he chose after visiting Europe. F. W. paid for the building in cash and a series of humorous caricatures in the lobby depicts the owner, the architect and the builders exchanging the building for money. See **WALK 4**.

World Trade Center: The twin towers of the World Trade Center dominate the skyline of Manhattan (see **A-Z**). The main attractions are the two observation areas in No. 2 World Trade Center, the south tower, which offer breathtaking views of the city, especially just before dusk when Manhattan gradually changes into a giant kaleidoscope of lights. At the top of No. 1 World Trade Center is the famous Windows on the World Restaurant which is very expensive, but serves excellent food and has the best wine list in America. See **SKYSCRAPERS**.

Zoos: *Central Park Zoo* - reopened in 1988 after a $35 million renovation, the zoo now boasts three ecological areas: the Tropics Zone, the Temperate Territory and the Polar Circle all set around a central formal garden. Walkways connect the indoor/outdoor habitats with the Sea Lion Pool in the middle. See **WALK 1**.
Bronx Zoo - the world's largest zoo with almost 4000 animals inhabiting 265 acres. Jungle World is the naturalistic habitat for Asian wildlife which can be visited by monorail on the Bengali Express. Don't miss the feeding times for the pelicans, crocodiles, sea lions, penguins and big cats. Try to visit in spring and summer when it is at its best. You can reach it on the BXM11 bus from Madison Av or by Metro North train from Grand Central Station (see **Railways A-Z**). See **CHILDREN**.
There are also zoos at Barrett Park on Staten Island (see **A-Z**), in Prospect Park (see **PARKS**) in Brooklyn (see **A-Z**), and at Flushing Meadow Park in Queens (see **A-Z**).